This book is de ██████ ster Lucia, without ██████ nt and persistence, it wou ██████ een written.

"...*there are as many forms of love as there are moments in time."*

Jane Austin

The Art of Moving in France

by

Angela Baggi

First Published in 2017

CONTENTS

-

- UNE BELLE DECOUVERTE

The Wrong House in the Right Location

- THE RIGHT HOUSE IN THE WRONG LOCATION

Home Sapiens?

- TOWARD UNCHARTED TERRITORY

The Principal Menace Identified

- DORDOGNE IS NOT WHAT IT SEEMS

The Village that is more British than French

- THE VILLAGE BETWEEN THREE
  DEPARTMENTS

A Sacré Transformation

- THE DIE IS CAST

The Cat that Sees Itself as a Tiger

- ON THE LAVENDER ROUTE

A Room with a View

- A WARRIOR MONK ON THE MOVE

To Find it, You Have to Know it is There

-

- REPETION OPENS DOORS

The Damned Village

- A COUNTRY WITHIN A NATION

A Lighter Shade of Bleak

- A VARIATION ON ANOTHER THEME

Farming is a Hopeful Occupation

- THINGS CHANGE TO STAY THE SAME

The Return of The Jedi

THE UNWITTING START OF THE JOURNEY

Les Alpes-de-Haute-Provence

The surge of spontaneity that prompted me to come and live in France in 2005, triggered a series of events that on hindsight could have easily been avoided, had it not been for the desire to find the perfect place in which to finally lay down my suitcases. Not only have I not found that place but am now even more convinced that it does not exist. The ideal place is where we have chosen to be and yet it can change the instant we have a deep insight into something; a thought or an awareness which reminds us that in effect we take the yearning for the perfect place wherever we go. One of the things I learned, after 15 moves in 12 years, is that it is not necessarily and always the location that makes one feel at home but one's attitude in relation to it. In revisiting all the properties I bought and sold, I feel an indelible fatigue and also a feeling of incredulity as if it has all been a wild dream. Could I have done something different in those twelve years, something that would have attributed more significance to my life? The answer is certainly yes, but it is what I chose to do and our choices bring us closer to knowing ourselves better.

The peregrinations started with a near-ruin in Montblanc, Les Alpes-de-Haute-Provence, that I bought after Michel and I separated the first time. I often thought about having a house in France, Provence in particular for it was the region I knew best and it vaguely resembled Tuscany, where I had been living for twelve years and found its landscape very appealing. Finding a house in Provence would have actualised my objective at that time but also served as an ostensible reason for reconnecting with Michel; I often experienced a lingering feeling that I had unfairly dismissed him after the failure of our brief attempt at living together. Michel was originally from Lille but escaped from the gloomy North and settled in sunny Provence several years before, built his 12m boat from scratch and sailed around the Mediterranean for twelve years. We had met on the Tuscan coast through a common friend. The event that stimulated my curiosity about Michel was a telephone message I had received from him, though he did not have my number – apparently. Ilaria, our mutual friend, swore she never disclosed my mobile to him and Michel likewise insisted he did not have it. I had erased the message because that voice was foreign to me - not just because of the French accent - and thought it was a wrong number. But I remembered the words; 'you have called for me and I have come, I am here for you,' and when we eventually met, I recognised his voice from the message. To this day there has not been a plausible explanation for that call.

Not long after we became acquainted, Michel moved in with me and sold his boat. He felt like a fish out of water and I, like a convenient stand-in; not a successful formula for a pristine relation. After a couple of months of fitfully awkward cohabiting, I showed him the door and he went to stay with his brother on the French West Coast. Whatever his defects may have been, he was incredibly talented; he painted delightful watercolours – which I had personally seen – and he could put his hands to anything including masonry, electricity, plumbing and carpentry, and this I had to take his word for it. During our separation, it occurred to me that Michel was probably feeling as if he lost his compass and that life on terra firma must be difficult to get used to after so many years on the water. All the more so because his hopes in a promising relationship had been dashed. What he sorely needed was a new project. And in that moment so did I.

My finances were very limited and could only afford a run-down stone house on the back mountains of the French Riviera so one day, with only a vague idea of what was available, I drove to the Alpes-de-Haute-Provence, fully confident I would find what I was looking for. Being a persistent type, I usually get results. I went into an estate agency in Saint-André-les-Alpes; it was there that I found the house. It was cheap, derelict and remote but it was old, in stone and full of sun; happily, it was selling at a price it would enable me to pay for the renovation costs as well. It was such an insignificant piece of real estate that the agent did not even go with me, he just handed me a piece of paper with the address of a neighbour who had the key and told me to go and find it. I did not blame him; he must have had more succulent deals to run after instead of racing off into the mountains with a woman whose determination he was not able to fathom. The neighbour was charming and informative; it was not clear whether she was trying to put me off or being helpful when she told me the man living in the valley below was an alcoholic and had a pack of Siberian Huskies who were incredibly noisy at night; she also said there were snakes and scorpions crawling all over the place. Before there was time to ask she added that she lived there because, despite the crawlers, she preferred the mountain life to living on the Coast where she came from, and hated with a passion. Whilst I was still riding on the wave of surged spontaneity, I decided to make an offer. The agent was surprised but happy to have earned a day's work without exerting himself. I returned to Italy and after a couple of months I was the owner of the house.

The process of buying and selling in Italy was familiar to me but not in France; however, my familiarity with the Latin judicial system was going to assist me in understanding French Civil Law. Notaries practise the same functions even if conveyancing may differ in minor details from one country to another. Italy being an extremely bureaucratic country with a complex judicial system packed with antiquated regulations is so incredibly slow in dealing with all administrative matters that it would make France seem like plain sailing by comparison.

These photos show how it looked after some works had already been done.

Whilst back in Italy, the thought of the house in Provence was present in my mind as was the question of what to do with it. After a while I got in touch with Michel and told him about my acquisition. Surprisingly he was very keen to get involved in my future plans concerning the house. The feeling that there was something unfinished between us had been nagging me and thought that perhaps I had wrongly estimated him. How we were thrown together when we met was not the most favourable of situations for encouraging a new relation to blossom. Relationships can have many forms and expressions; we may not have made a winning couple but that did not mean we could not be friends. We discussed the project and he was enthusiastic about moving back to Provence and start the renovation. Water and electricity were quickly activated and he could live in the house whilst carrying out the work. The fact that Michel was French was certainly an advantage as he knew how things were done though he vehemently disliked anything to do with bureaucracy and administration.

I was busy working in Tuscany at the time so I could only go to the house whenever a short absence from my work could permit it. More importantly I had to continue earning money in order to pay for the renovation costs, Michel's maintenance as well as my normal expenses in Italy. The distance between us was creating problems though. Installing a phone in the house was not easy to start with and it was essential if we were to communicate at all as the mobile did not work on the mountains. Twelve years ago we may not have been as dependent on internet as we are today but it had been habitual and essential to my work for several years and at that

time would have been the fastest and most
convenient means of communicating with
Michel. However, that was not possible yet as
there was no internet access at all, so we had to
be content with a landline but all the paperwork
had to be put in the post which was alas
predictably slow.

Michel had installed a septic tank, put a
bathroom in and created a bedroom on the first
floor, as well as other works that enabled him to
live in the house reasonably comfortably. I
worried about him being alone on the mountains
and having no one to help him with the heavy
work but I soon realized that he could very well
manage and had made a few friends in the
vicinity. I was introduced to them when I went
over and was pleasantly surprised at their
amiability though I suspected Michel was the
primary beneficiary; I was merely basking in his
popularity. Nobody knew who I was or what I
did, all they detected was that I was a foreigner
and the financer of the project; they probably saw
me as the unfair exploiter of a good hard-

working bloke who was the true owner of the house because it was he who was knocking himself out trying to make it liveable. It was not easy to deal with all the paperwork from a distance and as everything was in my name it seemed convenient to give Michel power of attorney so he could sign documents. The bank account I had opened in the local village was proving very useful in settling all bills.

I wished I could wind up my work in Italy and live in France all the time. On one of my visits Michel and I had a terrible row which ended badly and seemed unfixable. We were both tired and by the time I arrived, my long drive from Tuscany invariably put the final blow on an already weary physical and mental state. We decided – or rather I decided – to sell and separate once more. By this time, the house was looking good; I had spent a month decorating, painting and furnishing it and doing my best to make the garden look attractive knowing that what I planted in the summer would not necessarily survive in the winter as the Provence mountain areas are subject to drastic alternations in temperature. The water was supplied by a natural source and it was excellent but I sometimes wondered if it would ever dry up and we would be left waterless. Even if we had not separated I was not sure that was the place I would have lived in for any length of time so I was relatively happy to sell and go back to Italy – for the time being anyway. I had already moved my furniture and belongings into the house at a substantial cost and now they would have to be transported back to Italy again. The house was sold in a fairly short time, Michel's work was settled, and I went back to Tuscany though I knew that was not my final goodbye to France. This was in 2004.

My work was not going that well at the time and
my life in Italy was mostly unsatisfactory,
principally because of the politics and way in
which the welfare state was handled. Poor social
services, financial injustice - ministers are paid
three times the European equivalents plus
privileges whereas normal jobs are heavily taxed
and penalised – and having to tolerate a State that
is mistrustful of its citizens and yet does not
allow itself to be questioned. These and other
inequities succeeded in leaving me in a constant
state of exasperation and stress. Knowing full

well I was not going to change the status quo, the only alternative left to me was to leave. After many weeks, Michel and I started exchanging emails again and a few months later I decided to wind up my work and go to live in France. Michel had found a small – tiny in fact – place to rent not far from the house I sold. I stored my belonging in a garage in Italy and just brought what I needed to live in such a compact place and my dog Alba, of course, who always accompanied me everywhere. The exterior was very pleasant and had marvellous views over the valleys but the interior – it must have been no more than 35sqm – was going to be very challenging for two people and a German shepherd to live in. I moved in May 2005 and spent the first months painting watercolours and oils and making new acquaintances. Looking back now, it seems incredible that two of us and a large dog lived in that minuscule space for nearly a year even if we were out a lot.

One later afternoon I went to pee in the miniature shower room and when I flushed the toilet I noticed a large snake curled up on the tank lid. It was long, beautifully coloured and it looked peaceful and content but it still made me jump; I must have been very distracted not to have noticed it when I sat on the loo. What did I do? I called Michel and with a stick we managed to force the snake outside. We were told that when there is one, usually there are others nearby. It did not come in through the door, it entered from the cellar behind the bathroom wall. We discovered there was a hole in the wall (though it was baffling how it got through that narrow passage) that connected to the toilet tank water piper so we filled that hole and no more snakes came to visit. In French they are called *couleuvres* and as long as one cuts the grass they do not usually approach habitations unless they look for water, especially during the hot season. They are not poisonous but they can bite if seriously provoked or attacked.

Summer went by with long days spent by the Lac de Castillon in search of cooler climates; under the huge linden tree reading a book and falling asleep and sharing cool glasses of Bandol with friends at sunset. By the autumn, the need for a new project began to make itself be strongly felt. In truth, the idea of renovating another house had always been at the back of my mind and now was the right time to put the plan into action. Apart from having to tidy up some loose ends relating to my work in Tuscany, there was nothing on the horizon that promised to keep us occupied in a productive way in the coming winter. So, I set the wheels in motion.

TO THINK IT, IS TO CREATE IT

The Marvellous Feat

One day I was looking at the estate agent's window in the local village and saw a ruin being sold in a place called La Croix-sur-Roudoule, at a price I could afford. They generally say that when envisaging a renovation, one should plan to spend double the amount of the purchase price but in the case of a ruin such as that I knew it would end up being a lot more. That is why the purchase price had to be low. It should have been much lower had it not been for the fact that it was in Provence, the most expensive French Region. I discussed it with Michel and he told me he would only do the renovation if when it was sold he would get half the profit of the sale money. I agreed to this which seemed reasonable to me and so began the most incredibly audacious and dexterous project I have ever done.

The first thing to do was to get the water and
electricity connected which we did without

difficulty. It was simply a matter of paying. The local *Maire* (Mayor) was very helpful with the water and generally with the paperwork. The fact that someone had the courage to restore that decaying wreck, was not only beneficial to the local council but would also enhance the neighbourhood. By the time we started the renovation it was March so the weather was slowly improving though in that particular hollow part of the mountains it was rather damp and cold in the mornings until the sun was high enough to cover the whole area. The next thing to do was to empty it of all the rubbish that was left inside and outside which had to be taken to a *déchetterie* – recycling damp, that took up a lot of time because there was a huge amount of assorted scrap including metal, glass and plastic. It took me days to remove broken glass bottles buried in the earth around the house. It seems that when there is an abandoned spot with waste, people use it as a dumping ground for their own garbage without it ever occurring to them that someone will have to clean it up. In front of the place there was a large house which had been used as gîtes and was lived in by the owners who were extremely sympathetic to our project and daily stared at us as if we were out of our minds. The place – which was more a shed at that stage than anything resembling a home, with just a room upstairs where people slept judging by the number of beds – was so dilapidated and desolate that every morning when I arrived I had to ignore it and imagine the finished picture in my mind to avoid feeling despondent. Later, when I found out there were once copper mines in the area, it seemed evident the ground floor was used as a workshop and the miners slept upstairs. The roof had to be rebuilt as it was almost non-existent, the walls were slightly modified and we built a small *dépendance* in the garden. No permit was required if it was less than 20sqm. It was going to be used as a studio as we both painted and we needed a place where to store our tools and pictures. As wood was not expensive, the best way to heat the house was with a wood-burner but we wanted central heating and so we searched for a wood boiler which we finally found on the Côte d'Azur; I nearly smashed one of my fingers in the process of helping Michel transporting it and almost fainted from the acute pain.

I was adamant in finding someone to help Michel with the roof work despite him insisting he wanted to do everything on his own. Moving heavy beams at a certain height is not the kind of thing I was going to allow him to do on his own but it was a battle persuading him to accept help from a local French guy who had some building experience. According to Michel they shared no personal affinity and he did not like him. I told him it was not intended to be a long-term relationship and there was no time to try and find someone who could fulfil both requirements, that is; be competent in his work and compatible with his personality, and so he belatedly accepted. I could tell there was friction between them but it did not worry me for they were grown up men and their common sense would prevail.

Alba, my German shepherd, died just when we
started the renovation which in a way was a
blessing because having to cope with a hectic
agenda helped me manage the grief and sadness I
felt in losing her. She had been suffering from

hip dysplasia and she could hardly move; she was too heavy for me to lift her into the car and Michel did not like that dog breed so I had no help from him. The vet told me to give her some pills for her disease but they caused her to vomit and soon after developed pancreatic cancer. Alba was clearly suffering and wanted to crawl in a dark corner all the time. I really felt she was trying to tell me 'please let me go.' When she stopped eating I was obliged to take her to the vet and let her go. She was buried in the forest on the mountains amidst the wild flowers and the gentle breeze. It was a terrible time for me, she had been my friend for 12 years, so loyal, intelligent and affectionate, one could not wish for a better companion. Had there not been a project that demanded my total energy and attention, I do not know what I would have done.

We worked tirelessly every day and drove back to our little hut barely able to walk into the shower. Every morning, around 6am, I prepared our lunch, slogged all day and in the evening I had to get some supper ready as well as trying to keep the morale high and never show a decrease in enthusiasm. Spring definitely arrived on the mountains and the structure of the house was now solid but the walls needed pointing and windows and doors needed installing. What kept me going was the enthusiasm and trust in the success of the project but there were moments when I could easily have broken down and cried. Michel's weariness was obviously visible but was triumphantly camouflaged by his passion for the venture. After three months of gruelling activity I told Michel we were going to take complete breaks from the project at least once every two months otherwise we risked cracking up. So I organised trips to Paris, Cornwall and Amsterdam. They were too fugacious of course but they did help in providing distraction and temporary relief.

All materials for the renovation were bought in Nice (mostly from Leroy Merlin) and Michel's Pick-up proved very useful in transporting all sort of things. As money was going out all the time and none was coming in, (renovation costs are always higher than foreseen, especially in the case of a stone-built ruin) I decided to sell my Land Rover which was fairly new, and use the money to complete the renovation. Instead I bought an old Renault 5 for 300 euros that had been used by the EDF – electricity and gas supplier - some years back. It was blue and was totally mechanical and almost primitive but if anything went wrong with the motor, even I could fix it. It had no radio, no AC – nothing; I did not even lock the doors as there was nothing to steal, unlike the Land Rover that was completely electronic and had been broken into in Nice at least three times. The house was progressing rather well and as the word got around the valley, people used to stop and look at us incredulously whilst we were working. It was not easy to know what went through their minds as the French are seldom open about their thoughts and even though they may think it, they very rarely express admiration or praise. They do not however hesitate in being condemnatory and fault-finding. I imagined they were amazed at our courage and resourcefulness but there was no way of knowing for sure. After we put in the windows and the doors, the place was beginning to feel like it could be a proper home.

Not far from the house there had been copper mines because the mountains are full of the mineral. They are made of sedimentary rock formed by the deposition of successive layers of clay in warm red ochre. The mines are no longer active but there is now a museum with a couple of B. & B. attached. I made several trips up the mountains to collect big rocks – which nearly staved through the bottom of the Renault with the weight – for building a stone wall along the mountain road on the western side. We tried to utilise as much local materials as possible and as a small gate was needed for the garden, we decided to use boxwood which was plentiful higher up the mountains. I nearly ruined what was left of my hands in stripping the bark from the boxwood (it needs to be done soon after it has been cut from the tree to avoid bacteria seeping into the wood) but the end result was a superb and natural looking gate, thanks to Michel's able and creative hands.

The first winter we spent in the house was long and cold but the wood boiler provided an excellent central heating. The only snag was that it needed someone to charge the wood all the time and we could not leave the house for more than a day otherwise the temperature descended rapidly. The sun only shone on the property a few hours in the early afternoon from the end of October until April but after that things took on a more balmy and cheerful feel. It is a known fact that Provence is the sunniest region in France and it is quite true, even if one lives in the *arrières pays*, the only difference is that it is cooler than on the Coast. My French was not improving at all despite the fact that I had now been living in France for nearly two years. There was more than one reason for this; I had no time to concentrate on the language, no opportunity to meet anyone other than shop vendors and Michel insisted in speaking to me in Italian despite my frequent objections. He had learned the language when he was living on his boat in Italy and did not want to forget it; furthermore, I suspect it was easier for both of us since if we spoke French I would be asking for explanations and he would be wondering what I said. In our circumstances, we needed to simplify life and reduce unnecessary stress. The fact was that when the renovation was finished my grasp of the language was the same as when it began.

I always wondered if my poor French was the reason why when I went to any place like the Bank or the hardware stores people always spoke to Michel and never even glanced at me. The women smiled at him and said bonjour but they barely looked in my direction and when I paid the bill they would gape at me with disdain. Surely, they did not know if I spoke French badly or perfectly for I never had a chance to open my mouth save to say bonjour. It used to irritate me immensely, especially when I was in the Bank; it was my account, my money and my questions but they insisted in addressing themselves only to Michel. It was around about that time that I decided French men are considered gods in their country and women their appendages. Men are forgiven for everything; they can wheel-and-deal, steal and insult, lie and cheat, piss against public walls and behave indecently and get away with it whereas women would be condemned and severely criticised. Whatever high position they may occupy, it is never as high as that of their male counterpart. They are always kept in a kind of yielding, compliant mode. Having been brought up to be seductive creatures they are locked into an archaic version of sexual competition. Their enticing voices are used by advertising companies to lure people into buying products and their femininity is used by everyone exclusively in the pursuit of pleasure. A woman can have university degrees but she is often confined to lower-ranking jobs.

Rural economy of France had been largely supported and run by women; that is probably why despite earning half a man's wages for basically the same work, women were seen to have too much power and all anti-feminist reforms have always been so drastic. Married women had no right to control their personal properties and a wife's adultery was considered as serious as murder. Undoubtedly that is why many women decided to cohabit with a man without marrying him and concubinage was finally accepted in 1999 as a '*union de fait*' – legal union. Men are fundamentally afraid of women; they somehow perceive their power and have contrived ways to use them – sometimes abuse them – but always keep them under control.

Even today, in the male psyche, women fulfil only two roles, the sex symbol or the mother; the one who solves practical problems and forgives everything. Marianne may be a French symbol of Liberty but France is not ready yet to elect a woman as President of the Republic; it will be when both French men and women will have upgraded their opinion of women's acumen. All women who have been elected as Ministers have been severely criticised for one thing or another; men get away with murder. One thing has to be said though; women know how to exploit their gender. They want to secure their social, economic and political rights but they do not want to give up their advantageous position of being loved for their beauty, sexual power and allure. They are the queens of the bedroom and the terrors of public offices – *Le Service Public*. Wherever you go, whether it is a private company or a public office, you will almost always be confronted with sturdy women who always seem to be on the war path. They deal with all the paperwork, appointments and administrative tasks and provide a protective shield for men who occupy the high-ranking positions and who probably put in much less work than women. It is nearly impossible to get past these women; I have tried all types of subterfuges but then I am not Alain Delon.

The owners of the gîtes in front of the house, Odile and Marc, expressed their desire to sell their property; I was fairly sure it had nothing to do with us moving in the area! Having a large network of international contacts through my work, I offered to contact someone I knew in Amsterdam to see if he could come up with a buyer, even though the chances of it happening were very slim. However, he did come only once with a couple from London who, amazingly enough, decided to buy it. How the whole thing happened is a mystery still today, or an intuitive stroke of genius on my part, for having got in touch with my Dutch contact, and on his part for having procured the buyer. The owners of the gîtes – who have become dear friends and are still to this day – were thrilled to have got rid of that huge property that drained their energies and patience. They too were likewise dumbfounded and enthralled by the sale; they bought a sailing boat and drifted away toward new horizons on distant shores.

The second winter in that house was to be the last. The main reason was that having spent all the money in the renovation I did not see a way of improving my finances in such a secluded place. I had opened an atelier in the local village so that I could sell the few antiques left in my possession and my paintings but was forced to close it down after six months because Michel was hospitalized for an aneurysm and I decided to dedicate myself to looking after him.

In Nice, Michel was transferred to three different hospitals so I got to know all of them, though I would have preferred to have avoided the experience. Once I was asked if I could translate for a Danish woman whose husband was likewise in a coma due to an aneurysm; she did not speak any French and was anxious to know what was happening to her husband. They were on holiday in Nice and whilst in the swimming pool, her husband complained of a terrible headache. She got him some pain killers but it was too late, he passed out and had to be hurried to hospital. She told me her husband was a civil servant in Denmark and had not been under any particular stress, or had ever done any physical work but a doctor in one of the hospitals explained to me that it is not necessarily stress that can cause a brain haemorrhage, an artery can have a weakness from birth and one day, for many possible reasons, it ruptures and releases blood into the skull. The important thing is to be hospitalized as soon as possible and unfortunately Michel had remained a long time in that condition before the helicopter arrived from Nice. He was in a girlfriend's house at the time and though he complained of a headache she believed that was all it was. Only when Michel seemed to lose consciousness did she lift the phone to call me. I immediately contacted the SMU (Services Médicaux d'Urgence) who sent a helicopter in a nearby village and told me to take him to the doctor in a hurry whilst awaiting their arrival. Living on the mountains has advantages but also some drawbacks; driving him to Nice would have been an impossible and risky task to undertake.

When he finally recuperated after three months in hospital – the brain haemorrhage had forced him into a coma - I brought him home but things were not the same. Michel could hardly remember who I was. He needed to be taught how to swallow, speak, go to the lavatory - instead of peeing in the bed - be driven to the speech therapist and generally helped to rehabilitate. This he did in an incredible short span of time, even the doctors were amazed by his rapid recovery. His memory also improved but despite his fast recuperation, he could not paint again. Michel and I are in touch all the time and I have invited him in most of the places I have moved to since and I have been astounded by how his memory has improved, he remembers things that I have forgotten. However, something has happened to him, it is a subtle and indefinable change that is connected to his creativity and sensitivity. It is as if he has been stripped of a quintessence that constituted his uniqueness as a human being.

I was still exhausted from the renovation work and the driving up and down to Nice every other day in my R5 during the hottest months of the year and because Michel had never bothered to get his personal papers updated I had to get the *Assurance Maladie* (Social Insurance) to cover his illness one hundred per cent, apply for his pension and put all his documents in order. The task proved to be a sore test for my patience but also extremely educative.

I told Michel we had to sell the house because of financial difficulties and he agreed though I imagine for him it was an emotional shock. It was not clear whether he understood why we could not live on nothing but he probably did. It was round about this time that I received a letter from the French National Insurance telling me I was entitled to demand a pension. I had never thought about it and even if I had it would have been a huge dilemma to know who to ask and what to do. They offered to take care of everything for me both in UK and Italy; all I had to do was fill in some forms. As I had worked independently in foreign places where there was no by-lateral agreement, my pension would not amount to much but it would have been most welcome anyway. Those were the years when a woman could retire much earlier, had I waited a couple of years later it would not have been possible. What amazed me was that I started receiving my pensions (more than I expected) after three months and all I had to do was sign some documents. French efficiency was quite remarkable, it would have been a nightmare if I had to personally deal with the Italian and British National Insurances. Furthermore, they sent me a cheque for 800 euros for the contribution I made whilst I had the atelier, it was only six months so I doubt it amounted to that but it just showed how appreciative they are when someone takes a business initiative in a disadvantageous location. I do not know if it was the Nice Insurance Office that was so particularly effective or the French Insurance in general but it was certainly impressive.

I had no idea what the house was worth so I asked an agency to value it and it was much more than I expected and when I incredulously asked them if they had made a mistake in the valuation, they assured me that was the right price. Michel and I discussed it again and we agreed it had to be sold. Being on the mountains I assumed it would not be easy to sell; the road was winding and there were no amenities available. However, after a few months they came up with a buyer at a price that amply covered all my expenses, Michel's share of the profit and some left over for me. I found a place for Michel to rent in a hamlet in the vicinity and helped him furnish it. He was obliged to retake the driving test but he passed it and could be mobile again which was crucial for mountain life. The money in his bank account would make his life comfortable if he learned how to use it intelligently. Thus, one cold, snowy winter morning I dashed off in the freezing Renault 5 and headed in the direction of Avignon.

The Final Transformation.

THE JOURNEY TAKES A TURN

The City of Popes

After having lived in the middle of nowhere with no social life nor culture, I was instinctively drawn to a town but not just any town. I knew that in Avignon there was art, theatre, history and beauty. The *notaire* who drew up the contract in this purchase, was the most adorable one I have ever met. Had it been possible to use her for all my future contracts, I would have done so happily but notaries do not favour getting involved with properties in other regions as they may not be familiar with certain nuances in the transfer of ownership. The only thing I could afford in Avignon was an apartment; I had never lived in a new flat and it would not have suited me, it had to be something with character and a soul. I did find one very close to The Palais des Papes. It was on the ground floor, very small but in a 15th Century building and it even had a private courtyard. Naturally it needed renovating but after the recent magnum opus I had been through, it seemed like a piece of cake to me. The agency advertised it as 'habitable' but then anything that has electricity, water, a roof and upstanding walls is deemed habitable in France.

It needed refurbishing rather than renovating and I was living in the apartment whilst working in it. I had the kitchen and the bathroom redone by a professional and the rest I carried out myself. It did not take me very long to get the 'feel' of the place, the people and the ambiance. On the ground floor across the hall from me there was a young couple with a small dog who barked all day until he either collapsed from exhaustion or they returned from work. I offered to take him out for walks during the day but the girl said no. She had a habit of dropping the rubbish bag on the street in the evenings by opening her window which was large and very close to the pavement - being on the ground floor. Every morning the bags were spread all over the street – it was a narrow cobblestone medieval street lined by beautiful ancient buildings and listed as world heritage site by UNESCO – with paper, plastic and other rubbish flying everywhere. After tolerating this for a few days I stood outside one evening and caught her in the act. I asked if it was the local custom to put the rubbish outside the window and she replied '*Non, pourquoi*?' whilst giving me a vexed look. So I told her that I would happily take her rubbish to the bin (which was only 30 metres away) if she had no time because I did not find her habit very elegant. I knew full well this was going to turn her into an enemy. It will not be the first adversary I make in France but this was unexpectedly early and unforeseen. She had a pretty face but was overweight and emotionally unbalanced. I invited her *chez moi* for tea and surprisingly she came. She told me about the problems she was experiencing with her boyfriend; I offered my sympathy and genuine advice but I think it fell on deaf ears. She stopped putting the rubbish on the street and that was some small victory but her dog continued to exasperate the vicinage. It was not so much the noise that bothered me but the fact that the dog was locked up all day and I wished I could do something.

On the other side of my courtyard there was a tall avocado tree whose branches leaned partly into the small adjacent courtyard of the elegant Hotel attached to my building, and partly into my yard. I recognised it immediately when I moved because I once grew a small avocado tree by putting the stone in water until it developed roots. It surprised me that it could grow so big in a windy and, in the winter, bitterly cold climate. In fact, it was in a perfect spot, protected by high walls on all sides but not high enough to deprive it of sunlight. As the weather began to warm up and I could sit in the yard, I noticed it was full of avocados and they looked big and in perfect health. I knew the avocado is a climacteric fruit like the banana – it matures on the tree but ripens off the tree – and wondered if they were really mature. I must admit the thought of picking one crossed my mind but did not because I could not have reached that high and, more importantly, the tree did not belong to me. However, one day a violent gust of Mistral blew several avocados on the floor. I picked them up and noticed they were not yet ripe but would soon be, especially if I put them near some apples. I went out in the street and rang the ground floor bell of the house that according to my calculations was the proprietor of the tree but there was no answer so after some deep thinking I decided to give some to my neighbour, some to the Hotel, and keep two for me. When I ate one it brought me back to a similar experience; the first time I savoured a locally grown papaya when I was in India. The taste was quite different from the fruit one buys in the supermarkets; it was as if I tasted that fruit for the very first time. There was even a unique fragrance in both the papaya and the avocado, which is totally lacking in industrial productions. Strange how we never forget certain tastes and smells, they leave an impression that colours all our future experiences.

I spent my days visiting museums, libraries, art galleries and parks, as well having some delicious meals in chic restaurants. I also wrote some articles for a local paper and joined a French-conversation class. It was a novel experience to walk outside and be a stone's throw away from everything. But the thought of moving began to cross my mind. There were several reasons for this. One was that the couple above me slept all day and lived by night. As I was about to go to sleep they would put the loud music on and start cooking at 1100pm inflicting the smell of garlic- that I hardly tolerated at daytime let alone when I was going to sleep - on the whole neighbourhood. I did not say anything because I did not want to make another enemy just yet and in any case, they were not going to change their habits or move elsewhere just because of me. The other reason was that my living room had a ventilation grid that connected to the cellar and there was frequently a dreadful sewage smell coming up, especially when it rained or was windy. After some investigating it transpired that the sewage in the building was not yet connected to the mains and was still dependent on a septic tank. This discovery shocked me and even though the *syndicat de copropriété* assured me it would be connected within a few months I did not believe them and furthermore I was not prepared to sit through the wait and then the changeover. It was understandable that in a city like Avignon it was not easy to convert ancient buildings to the main sewage but it was also unbelievable that it had not yet been done. They certainly had plenty of time to do it since all the sewage freely flowed into the Rhône. Pretty much the same as the river Arno collected all the city discharge well before and after the Ponte Vecchio was inhabited by butchers. Nowadays, the Ponte Vecchio hosts prestigious jewellers and Florence, just like Avignon, has become a renowned tourist destination and fancies itself as the epitome of charm and elegance. It is really a case of appearances can be deceiving and appearances in France are very important, as they are in Italy where they have an expression for this; *bella figura*. It means that they put much careful attention on how they appear to the outside world but what is seen is not necessarily what is unseen. *Figura* in Italian means the form of things (like a well-shaped woman) but also the appearance and presentation. I told myself that perhaps it is a Latin characteristic because in the South people spend more time outdoor than indoor and appearances are very important. I did not doubt there was a good technical reason and did not so much mind that the sewage was not connected to the mains as the fact that I should have been told when I bought the flat. Some people would have made a fuss about this blunder but I chose to leave instead. So I put the flat up for sale and voilà I found a purchaser after a month. (I have sold almost all my houses within two months).

The buyer was a journalist from Paris who kept saying '*j'adore, j'adore!*' every three minutes and wanted to buy it as quickly as possible. I told her about the sewage but not about the neighbours, after all they may have changed by the time she moved in or she may have a totally different experience of them than I had. I recovered the money I invested in the flat and made some profit on the furniture the woman wanted to buy at all costs so everything turned out well. I made the most of Avignon while I was still there as I knew that was probably going to be the last time I would live in a town or a city.

There are certain advantages but also many drawbacks and for me the latter outweighs the former. I invited Michel to come and stay for a week and he was delighted to be able to go to the cinema, restaurants and art galleries without having to take the car.

And so I started searching for my next dwelling in a small village and this time it had to be a house as living in an apartment was not going to work. I liked the Vaucluse and was not quite through with it but prices were high and my spending capacity was low. Finally, I found a terraced house in Roaix, a village just over 40 kms north of Avignon. The landscape there is stunning; vineyards and hills with the Mont Ventoux in the distance offer a variety of truly beautiful sceneries. There are some character villages pertaining to the denomination of '*Les Plus Beaux Villages de France*,' such as Séguret, and of course renowned wines such as Châteauneuf du Pape. In Italy, as an example, there are excellent wines and villages – though one must admit that villages are more pieces de résistance in France whilst in Italy towns are more interesting – but the French know how to market and sell their properties and products and have no qualms in calling them 'the most beautiful,' 'divine,' or 'sublime.' And, of course, they really believe they are. Italians have a wealth of richness in architecture, art and products but they would never dream of calling them the most beautiful, divine or sublime. Perhaps it is true that if someone believes in something hard enough, they make it real. At least for those who believe it anyway.

Vineyards near Villedieu, Vaucluse

UNE BELLE DECOUVERTE

The Wrong House in the Right Location

The house I bought did not really need serious
renovation and once more it was sold as
'habitable et rénovée' but as it had been lived in
by a single father with two children what it really
needed was elbow grease and redecorating. The
fact that it was on the road worried me somewhat
even if at that time I had no pets. I was concerned
by the traffic and knowing that getting a truthful
answer out of neighbours would be a waste of
time, I did not even bother to ask if there was
heavy traffic passing through the village. Even in
a small hamlet often there are farmhouses or
animal breeders on the outskirts which means
that tractors and *camionnettes* or lorries go
backward and forward all day and this I was not
to know - yet. The chateau that was once part of
a Commandery of the Knights Templars was
interesting but its gardens with the lily pond,
even more so. The owner, who was occupying
the castle spasmodically, had instructed the

caretaker to allow some people to visit and I was lucky to be one of them. I moved there in the spring of 2008 and started redecorating immediately.

Summer came and as the house was south-facing, the heat became so unbearable in July and August, I had to install an air-conditioner. It was an old stone-house with thick walls but all the rooms were exposed to a daily dose of at least 30 degrees and even solid walls have their limits. I had lived in the Middle East for many years where heat was much more intense but all buildings were so cool inside it was easy to forget it was hell outside. I spent my time indoor painting and writing with the occasional walk early morning and even exhibited my paintings in Avignon. I met some lovely people in the village who are still friends today though I have not seen them for a while. In Vaison-la-Romaine there is a wonderful market every Tuesday which did impress me. My experience of markets in France had been disappointing, especially in Provence where some people tried to sell me stuff they claimed was genuine *provençal* when in fact it is mass produced in a Slovenian factory, and so it was refreshing to find authentic products from the area at decent prices. I went to Mont Ventoux a few times just to savour the magnificent view from the top and in the autumn walked around the vineyards and admired the shades of gold and green gleaming with sunshine. But I was getting itchy feet…

One of my habits is to photograph a house as soon as all the works have been done – naturally on a sunny day. It occurred to me that I subconsciously want to be ready to go and do not wish to be caught off guard. The fact that I had not 'transformed' the house but merely redecorated it, was not going to make it a profitable sale, perhaps not sell at all, unless I put it at the same price I bought it. I asked an agency to give me an estimate and they confirmed what I thought except the price would include the money I had spent on it. This reassured me and to avoid increasing the price by adding a hefty commission on top I advertised the house myself. It only takes one, they say, and that is what I kept reminding myself when nobody called in response to my advert. Until one day, two months later, a woman called, came and bought it.

Sales procedure usually takes two to three months depending on the notary's speed, the attainment of necessary documents and whether there is a mortgage or not. I have been known to complete after one month of the preliminary signature but it is unusual. My problem was that I had to synchronise the sale with the purchase of the next property and avoid having to rent in the meantime. I thought about the possibility of renting but my income was insufficient. This meant that I could only choose from what was for sale in that particular moment and within my budget. This is one of the reasons why my searches extended to other regions in France. I would have liked to stay in Provence but the price I could afford enabled me to purchase either a dilapidated place or in a God forsaken location, neither of which options was attractive to me at the time. So I turned my gaze to Languedoc; it was still the South and the choice of reasonably priced properties was much more interesting. I looked on internet first and selected a small number of houses to visit. In general that is how it goes. Since I dislike looking at properties anyway and in particular wasting my time and that of others, I always search on internet first – this can take hours – and once I have picked a few, I ring the agents or the owners to get more information and answers to my questions. They often lie, regardless of whether they are agents or private owners, so it takes a certain amount of insistence and Machiavellian craftiness but with practice my skills have improved. Once made the appointments, the trip is organised and, mainly by necessity, my faith in a positive result is regenerated. I was leaving Roaix with a certain sadness in my heart; a place I knew and liked; friends nearby, and I was going to an unfamiliar and unexplored location. Roaix may not be on the list of 'Les plus Beaux Villages de France' but it is still a little beauty.

Roaix

THE RIGHT HOUSE IN THE WRONG LOCATION

Homo Sapiens?

I found a property in a village called La Livinière in the department of l'Herault. It had been renovated by the owners who were a retired couple from UK. I was going to discover that if a house has been renovated by British owners it is normally well done and one is unlikely to find negative surprises. The same is not always true for the French. The estate agent and the notary were both women and both snooty and unpleasant but luckily our association was very brief and temporary. From this encounter I was to learn another lesson; avoid meeting notaries where possible by signing a power of attorney; that minimises tension. If you buy for the first time and only once in twenty years it does not matter but once a year, as it was visibly going to be for me, then it is another story. I admit that my frankness and upfront personality do not always go gown well. I cannot stand hypocrisy and pretence (does anyone?) and do nothing to hide it. This is obviously not a favourable feature in France.

It is almost impossible to be aware of all the information when buying a property; the house itself could hide irregularities which even if they were known to the agent or the notary they would not necessarily disclose them, (even if the notary has an obligation to do it) the neighbours could be from hell; the future council's building and urban plans – like the expropriation of a property or the building of a road – could devalue the property, and so on. There is no survey done in France unless one arranges it independently and it can be expensive and finally unproductive. So one has to rely on intuition, expert observation and the diligence of the agent, or the owner, and the notary. The latter is totally unbiased and represents the State as opposed to a lawyer who represents the client. A notary has only knowledge of what is documented, he or she has never seen the property so they cannot know what it is like to live in it, if the toilet works or the neighbour plays hard rock at night; the agent knows the property but has only a superficial knowledge of the documents and the owner can always deny knowledge of certain hidden flaws. Speaking the language helps as does a certain amount of luck and explicit credence. I have met many notaries in France, some have been very meticulous and affable, some sloppy but simpatico, most of them are prima donnas and a couple are now my friends. Estate agents are generally competent and efficient but they can also be intimidating and pushy so one needs to be strong-minded. That is the main reason why they have a *délai de rétractation* in all the purchase contracts; ten days withdrawal period during which buyers can change their mind without any penalty whatsoever. At first I thought this clause was to allow for people's feebleness and lack of forethought but after meeting a number of estate agents I began to see the sense in it. In addition, some people have *a coup de coeur* (vague word with several interpretations but basically meaning love at first sight) for something and then regret having put their signature on it. I can see why some people prefer to find a property through an agent rather than negotiate with the owner directly, often at a considerable added cost. First of all, they feel more protected and secondly it is emotionally easier to deal with a neutral person. In my intense experience, I have bought from both; agents and directly from owners. If one buys from the owners all one has to do is to give the details of the owner and property to one's notary and then leave it to them to deal with everything. That is what estate agents do anyway so a commission is often a waste of money. We are obliged to buy through agencies because that is the only way to find a property for sale. If buyers are slightly nervous in buying directly from the owner, the same applies for the reverse.

The house was in a narrow street with a square in the vicinity where one could park which, I was going to find out, is a considerable advantage because in Languedoc everyone seems to be constantly competing for a parking right. It also had a house in front that at the beginning did not bother me but would later turn out to be something to be avoided. The village is renowned for its wine and it also has an excellent restaurant. The owners of a celebrated winery lived not far from me and as I got to know them they offered their *cave à vin* for an exhibition of my paintings. I did not really care for too much attention so I asked an English painter if she wanted to share the space with me. It turned out she was a much better artist than I - which is undoubtedly an easy feat - and sold several of her watercolours whereas I did not. But then that was her profession and she deserved to be appreciated whereas for me it was a hobby. Exhibiting in a wine cellar seems a good idea because it has more than one reason to be appealing.

As the heat began to increase, people in the village spent more time outside, especially in the evenings when it was cooler. There were no gardens or parks so they sat outside their houses in the street. That was the case of the people living in front of me. The kept quiet behind closed shutters during the day but they came alive from 9.00pm onward, as most of the southerners do. I go to bed fairly early and get up before dawn so by the time I was ready to read in bed and eventually fall asleep, they increased the volume of their voices and by 11pm they were in full swing. Sound tends to rise and from where I was I could hear every word they said so I was compelled to close my bedroom window which vexed me because it was then that one needed to open it, to cool the room. I tried the ear plugs and everything else I could think of but nothing presented itself as a solution. I even ventured out and joined them but their conversation was so tedious and miserly that it could not be sustained for more than once or twice. My attempt to badinage in French was a complete waste of time and any effort to elevate the quality of the conversation was a total failure. So, with mixed feelings and a certain hesitancy I decided to go and talk to the Maire to see if he could suggest something. He told me it was not permitted to make noises in the streets after 10.00pm unless it was an exceptional occasion – like Bastille Day -

and that he would talk to them. His words instead of sounding appeasing, as they should have done, sounded more like a menace. I knew the French sufficiently by now to realize that if the Mayor was going to tell them I complained to him, they would become resentful and the extent of their recrimination was going to reveal itself to me very soon. I was to discover that the French can put up with the most intolerable things from neighbours without ever complaining because they are afraid of retribution. They may write anonymous letters but never manifest themselves openly. It is a sort of contradiction because it has been said the French are quarrelsome by nature and yet they are incredibly tolerant. It occurred to me that village life is something they have experienced for many centuries and are masters at it. The only way they can be free to do what they want is to allow others to do the same without grumbling.

Boredom is one of the main elements for social unity. Perhaps it has been a notable force that counteracted the effects of poverty and, more significantly, it brought people together. Boredom led them to test each other, form ménage à trois, invent strange beliefs and legends and has been one of the tenets of French society. When someone new moves into a hamlet or a village, the locals will have already formed an imagined interpretation of that person, even before they ever meet. That mental image being different in each of them, according to their acumen, ability to imagine and degree of boredom, will now become the topic of discussion during many monotonous village conversations.

The noise not only increased and extended to midnight or later but suddenly the whole neighbourhood stopped saluting me. The hostile atmosphere became unbearable and I did not know how to improve it; the damage was done and the only solution was to sell and leave. The house was small but as a second home it was perfect. There was a terrace on the top floor, nothing to be done in the house and there was also a small dependence at the back of the house that I already began renovating.

I was not going to make any profit on this
house either because I had paid too much when I
bought it and the only changes I made was to

repaint the shutters and change the front door, as well as minor cosmetic works and some improvements in the small barn at the back. I put an advert myself and once again did not get much feedback but one day, nearly two months later, a couple from Belgium came and seemed to like it. They said they would go and walk around the village and perhaps come back so I did not think I would see them again but they did return and made an offer. I could have waited and tried to get more but as long as the selling price covered all my costs, which it did, it seemed a good idea to accept. Whilst waiting for the notary to deal with the sale, I started thinking about where to go next. I needed a renovation project as the last two houses were already done and I prefer to do restoration myself. Even if someone has done a good job, it is never exactly as one would have wanted it and it is too expensive to undo what someone else has done. But my experience of Languedoc – at least in that particular street, in that particular village – had been unpleasant and so to avoid southern habits it seemed apt to direct my search in the direction of the North.

In the meantime, I was called by an acquaintance in Béziers who worked for the SPA – Societies for the Prevention of Cruelty to Animals – inviting me to visit her as there were many dogs who needed a home. I told her I had a small house and no garden so I could not have a big dog as in the past and she said there was a small Terrier who was desperate for some love. So, despite my reluctance due to the sorrow I still felt in losing Alba, I went and voilà I came home with this little rascal.

He was called Caramel - as all animals of that reddish/beige colour are - for ease sake but to avoid confusion in the streets if he was to meet other Caramels, I called him Mel – later to become Mel the Braveheart, because he proved himself to be truly fearless. My life was never going to be the same again. It was my first experience in living with a small dog, and a Terrier, a particularly wiry and energetic dog. Whereas the first few days he behaved in a meek and contented manner, his real character began to manifest itself very soon. I did not know how I was going to handle such an active and demanding dog especially since I was getting older and was always busy with new projects. Mel was un-trainable and the only thing he could obey to was *'tu reste là'* which must have been inflicted upon him when he was a puppy by his original owners. After the obligatory visit to the vet and the resulting medical treatments – at a shockingly exorbitant cost – I settled to the fact that I was going to be stuck with him for the rest of his/my life. I was told he had been in a cage with two big dogs and obviously one of them had been sufficiently enraged to bite one of his ears, plus he coughed a lot and must have suffered hunger as he swallowed his food at the speed of light – and does to this day - without even considering chewing it. After a couple of months I was exhausted, Mel however was in perfect health and has become my new travelling companion.

TOWARD UNCHARTED TERRITORY

The Principal Menace Identified

On an online British website I found a house in
Charente-Maritime that caught my entire
attention. It was owned by an English woman
who used it as a holiday home and even if she
had it well camouflaged to look enticing, it was
clear to me it needed total renovation. It had a
garden which was now a desirable thing to have,
and was in a region that was north enough but
had the reputation of being sunny and temperate.
I waited for the withdrawal period to expire – as I
always do before looking for another property –
in case they changed their mind, and then
arranged my visits in Charente-Maritime. There
were a few properties I had planned to see
though I knew already that was the most suitable
house. It was shown to me by a friend of the
owner who had the keys and was also British. It
needed a full renovation but had an enormous

potential and hidden charm. The style of the house is called '*longère Charentaise*' and has the advantage of being single storey with large windows. There was also a large attic that could be converted into several bedrooms.

Marianne, the woman who had the keys of the house, told me that her son was a builder and her husband a DIY man so if I wanted they could take care of the entire renovation. This was extremely encouraging as not only I would not have to look for artisans but I would have to deal with Brits for a change. I gave her the list of works I planned to carry out and I was given an estimate very rapidly. I was amazed by how reasonable the cost was and wondered if they were any good. Two months later I went back to Charente-Maritime and signed the purchase contract. I rented a gîte not too far from the house, whilst the work was being done but to avoid putting my furniture in storage I had it delivered in the house and covered it with plastic sheets. I arrived in November and it was not the best time to begin a major renovation. The house was gelid and as there were two fireplaces, Leon, his father and brother-in-law started burning the old wood they demolished from the ceilings and the roof. It was a good idea in principle but what we did not know was that the old wood was full of woodworms and other parasites which the fire activated and caused to spread everywhere, even if they were not visible. As a result, I started itching everywhere and when I went back to the gîte I noticed I had a dreadful irritation all over my body with red patches that itched relentlessly. I could not sleep and spent my time scratching myself. Finally, I had to go see a doctor who gave me all sorts of antihistamine, anti-tetanus and antibiotic treatments; though why antibiotic was a mystery he could not explain. French doctors prefer to extirpate a disease rather than merely treat it. He said he had never seen anything like it and to know exactly what it was that caused it, the wood would have to be analysed but as there were probably hundreds of parasites living in old wood it would take a long time and we may not ever find the ultimate answer. Only the younger builder had a similar irritation albeit in a minor form. Even today the skin on my arms shows faint darker patches.

One important detail the vendor forgot to mention was that the house was not connected to the mains drainage, in fact all there was in terms of lavatory was a *fosse étanche* (pit toilet). When I visited the house she said there was a *fosse septique* (septic tank) which would have been marginally better but in reality it was an outside hut with a hole in the earth and that was it. That is what was once used but it was incredible that in 2009 it was still unchanged. It meant that the hole in the ground had to be emptied on a regular basis and, to make things worse, being extremely small and shallow, that had to be done every month, even if it was used by just one person, at the cost of 110 euros every time. The builders who knew the vendor, were so taken aback when they discovered the unpleasant surprise, they could not believe she never disclosed it. I immediately went to the Mairie and asked when they planned to connect the village to the mains and they promised it would be done within the year. We had the new bathroom done with the required pipes set up in readiness to connect to the mains. My weekly visits to the Mairie may or may not have helped in getting things moving but in September 2010, they finally did the connection, thus making life worth living again.

When I talked to a few French people about the state of the sewage, none of them seemed at all distressed or surprised, so accustomed were they to use a chamber pot (in some areas referred to as the '*Vicaire*') adopt a designated corner of the garden, put their feet on porcelain footpads on either side of a dark hole, or use sheltered places like bridges and covered alleys. They sold the dung to a manure collector and this is still done in Brittany, for example, even though it has been declared illegal.

That winter was really hard work for me. Buying the material, working in the house and supervising the renovation, driving backward and forward to the gîte, keeping my dog happy and getting to know local customs. The incredibly lucky thing was that the builders proved to be extremely capable, especially Leon, who was so skilful. He was not easy to communicate with but his intelligence and talent made up for it. The gîte I was staying in was owned by a British couple who lived in the main house. I was the only person renting one of the four gîtes. I insisted on the non-negotiable availability of wi-fi which they promised me there was but in reality if I wanted to use internet I had to go into another gîte and stay by the front door (where the signal was receivable) which considering the cost of the rental was unsatisfactory and even distressing. But at that point it was a fait-accompli for me, it would have been too difficult to find anything else so I was stuck with it. At Christmas time they went back to UK and as I was completely alone on the compound with nothing but empty fields and country lanes nearby, it was not exactly a welcoming environment so I invited Michel, who was also alone, to come and spend Christmas with me. One night there was a sounder of wild boars in the courtyard and that got me, and especially Mel, very animated. I had chosen that gîte for three main reasons; one was that it was not too far from the house I bought, second because it was a single storey (I had hurt my left meniscus and preferred to avoid stairs in case it got blocked) and finally because they accepted my dog. The other thing is that in the winter a lot of gîtes and B. & B. are closed so there was not really a vast choice.

Toward the spring, I moved into the house and although things ended badly between Leon's father and me – I was accused of being overbearing and tyrannical – I was so delighted to be in a house that was renovated according to my taste and with nobody in front that I forgot about the falling-out for a while. After putting in the final touches and furnishing it, I wrote a letter to Marianne asking her husband to excuse my seeming iron-fisted personality and hope I was forgiven though someone like her husband may have partly forgiven me but certainly not forgotten. He did not have a taste for being told what to do by a woman. To this day, I regret not having been more considerate and patient with them and even if I tell myself I was tired and stressed and wanted things to move faster, it does not help and it is no excuse for my lack of flexibility. They too were under pressure and working for me in a chilly environment. Of all the artisans I have encountered up to now, they remain the most skilful, honest and creative and would have even paid for their flight and rental just to have them with me in my future projects, if it were possible.

Spring was in full swing and the garden also needed taking care of as it had been neglected for a long while. I had neighbours on either side because it was a terraced house but at least they were not right in front and with a little screening it was possible to avoid running into each other too often. On my right, there was a Portuguese elderly man and on the left an elderly French woman and they, I later discovered, did not talk to each other. The thought of putting up a concealing fence occurred to me but it may have sent the wrong message so in the end I planted the sort of evergreen trees which embellished the garden and guaranteed some privacy on one side but had to put up a bamboo fence on the other side because the Portuguese neighbour lurked in his garden waiting for me to go out of the house and glare at me all the time. Every village in France has one or more persons who do not communicate with someone. Usually it is for a trivial reason but what is even more trivial is that none of them do anything to mend fences, even when they are so old they cannot remember why they do not talk to each other. Being curious by nature and disliking quarrels with a passion, I tried to find out why my neighbours were so guarded and hostile toward each other but it was too early to expect a response.

The house was very comfortable to live in. I liked the lovely whitewashed lime stones that had been pointed in almost all the rooms. The walls could have been insulated to make the house warmer in winter but it was a shame to hide such beautiful stones. The corner ones had been hand cut and are typical of that region where there were once many stone quarries and crafts. Being south-facing with large windows, the house was full of light even on a grey day. The church in the village – Eglise de Saint-Martin – is Romanesque and is the only interesting thing there though there are other villages in the vicinity, like Saint-Savinien and Crazannes (famous for its limestones) which are very charming and worth a visit. Coming from Tuscany and Provence, the flat landscape of Charente- Maritime seemed very monotonous and uninteresting but on the other hand there was a lot more sky to look at.

The relationship with my two neighbours developed to more than a 'bonjour' but I soon realized that what they liked to discuss was each other. She was telling a story and he another. I never tried to discover the truth as it was not of interest to me, besides I knew that if they talked to one another, they would each say something different about me. My impression was they were very keen to communicate but neither of them would take the first step to make that possible. I asked them if they needed anything whenever I went shopping and generally tried to be helpful but I sensed it was not going to be easy to reconcile them and finally put the thought out of my mind. All sorts of good and bad things happened to me in the short time I inhabited that house. In the village – as indeed in all French villages – there were stray cats and *comme d'habitude* I started feeding them at the back of the house trying to avoid being seen by Mel who has an aversion to cats. After a few months, I was approached by a strange woman who accused me of wanting to appropriate myself of her cats. I asked her why she did not feed them if they were her cats and she replied that they did not need feeding, they ate rats and what they could find in the rubbish bins. 'What happens when they give birth to kittens?' I asked. She told me they were killed if there were too many. There was no point in pursuing the conversation, it was only going to distress me so I reduced the amount and frequency I was feeding them and hoped for the best. After that unsettling conversation, I ran into that woman a couple of times but she did not salute me.

One day as I was walking my dog I noticed a *camionnette* parked along one of the side roads and heard a dog whining inside. On closer inspection I noticed that all the windows were closed and the dog was locked inside a cage in the minivan. As it was July and fairly hot I was worried the dog would die so I knocked on the houses nearby and asked who owned the van. Nobody knew who it belonged to; or rather they knew but would not tell me. Later I went to the Mairie and asked them who was the owner of the vehicle. They told me it was an old lady's nephew who lived two streets away and gave me the address. I immediately went to the house and the old lady confirmed it belonged to her nephew who was asleep because he worked at night. 'And does he leave the dog in the car all day with the windows shut ?' I enquired, sensing already that I was embarking on a dodgy mission. She just looked away but promised me she would tell him. When I went back later, nothing had changed. The next day I took the same road and found the same *camionnette* with the dog inside who was whimpering and I wondered how he or she could still be alive in that heat. I went back to the Mairie and expressed my concern for the animal; could they do something? They replied that the man was '*un peu spécial*' which – amongst other things - means bizarre but one never knows what exactly goes through their minds when they say it. They suggested to ring the SPA and they will handle the problem. So I did just that. They assured me I would remain anonymous and instructed me to ring them again the next day. When I called they said if I had delayed an hour the dog would have died. He was unable to walk because he was shut in the cage all the time except on rare occasions at night and they could not understand how he was still alive as he was suffering from severe heat stroke and malnutrition. 'You did a good thing,' they assured me. The dog was now in their care. A week later I found my car heavily scratched on both sides and it brought me to tears. It was a recent Skoda and was going to cost me a fortune to have it repaired. I knew without a doubt who was the malefactor as it was done in the village during the night. I told my neighbour, Jeannette, the French pensioner, and she said that is why people never report anything, because they are afraid of vengeance. She also warned me to be careful as he was a dangerous type. So everyone knows everything but nobody says anything, I thought to myself. One day I ran into him – or rather he was waiting for me where I usually returned from my dog walk – and he shouted *'salope'* (slut) and other equally offensive words at me in the street. I ignored him and walked on and wondered what else I should expect from him. However distasteful and distressing it had been I never regretted doing what I did to save the dog.

One very positive thing that happened to me in Charente-Maritime was meeting some lovely people who would become my friends. One was French and three were British. I had joined an artists' association and took part in three collective exhibitions, one on the Ile d'Oléron, another in Saint-Savinien and the third in Saintes. I sold an oil painting and was given a prize for a watercolour which naturally pleased me. During the exhibition in Saint-Savinien I met a British sculptor, Richard, who makes lovely statuettes with the Crazanne limestones and marble. He was trained as a scientist and when he moved to France he discovered his talent in sculpting and decided to stay. He and his wife Heather are dear friends now.

I also joined a dog group; this was run by some British dog-owners who met once a week to walk their dogs and then have tea in each other's houses. Mel was delighted to find company – the more the better as he is a very sociable creature. It was fun to walk with assorted people and dogs but the tea and coffee part lingered far too long and as I do not drink either I preferred to leave after the walk. There were some interesting people even if I did not bond with any of them. If I missed a week's walk with the group, Mel would look at me persistently as if to say, 'have you forgotten something?' There was a pretty Fox Terrier he had his eyes on and spent his time dancing for. Apart from the Beagles I had when I lived in London, my experience of male dogs was very limited, especially small male dogs. Mel had to be sterilised because he was so incredibly randy, dominant and even aggressive with other males that controlling him was proving to be a dilemma. It took me three visits to the vet before I made up my mind and when he said that it was for my dog's benefit and not detriment that he needed to be neutered because of his over-productive testosterone glands that caused him to be unhappy, I finally gave in. He also added that it would take a while after the operation to notice the difference in behaviour. It is now eight years later and Mel is still dominant and aggressive with non-sterilised males and still leaves his scent on most legs he finds.

A man knocked on my door one afternoon and came bearing a gift; it was a pot of honey that he made himself, or rather his bees had. I thanked him but was not sure if he wanted to be paid or not so I engaged him in a conversation about bees and asked him if he sold his honey. '*Non, non*!' he protested with indignation as if he had been asked to sell his soul. '*C'est pour moi seulement...et pour mes amis.*' I felt honoured to be counted among his friends and invited him for tea. We talked some more and when he left he asked if he could come back and visit me again to which I replied '*mais bien sur.*' After a couple of weeks he was back and this time he was elegantly dressed with a bunch of stooping flowers in his hand. Not assuming they were for me I offered to put them in some cold water and he thanked me. He apologised they were tired looking but he had walked a long way and he added that the flowers were for me. He told me where he lived and it was indeed a fair distance from my house so it was puzzling how he found me but he did not reply to my question. My French at the time was not as fluent as today and to avoid misunderstandings I always opted for short questions like '*pourquoi? comment? où*?' and preferred listening rather than talking. It became clear to me he wanted to establish some kind of friendship with me, or perhaps more than that and as I felt absolutely nothing for this man it was better not to give him any hope and then disappoint him. So, I told him I was single but liked my life as it was and had no intention of changing it. He seemed to understand but went off looking as if someone had thrown a bucket of cold water over him.

A very positive aspect of living in Charente-Maritime is its geographical location; towns like La Rochelle, Rochefort and Saintes, are full of history, charm and culture and at reasonable distances from each other. After Provence, Charente-Maritime is the *département* that has most sunshine though nowadays the weather is less predictable. It is in the region of Poitou-Charente (now forming part of Nouvelle-Aquitaine) and as you move away from the coast, the light dims somewhat, like a chandelier whose bulbs are not all lit. Unlike my dog, I am not gregarious and clubby but had I wanted to be a socialite, in Charente-Maritime I would have had plenty of opportunities to be. In fact, that was the major advantage of living in that village; being fairly close to Saintes, Rochefort, Royan, Saint-Jean-d'Angély and La Rochelle; the latter being a splendid city with a marvellous port. La Rochelle was founded as a city in the 10th century and became a free port in 1137; it became the property of Henry Plantagenet (Henry II) after two decades and was turned into a flourishing maritime commerce and trade port, mainly with England. It was also the Knights Templars' largest base on the Atlantic Ocean and vestiges of their Commandery can still be seen today. It is a city well worth visiting with a fascinating historical heritage.

In less than a year I had managed to do and discover many things. The house was too big for one person and as winter was approaching it was going to be expensive to heat so I began thinking about changing it for something smaller. There was plenty of space for guests but the only friends who came to visit were Michael, whom I had met in Languedoc, and Lizzy who came from London for a weekend. I had invested quite a bit of money in the renovation and hoped I could make a little profit which I badly needed and would have compensated my hard work. I had never been in Dordogne and knew it was a region full of magnificent fortified villages; medieval architecture being one of my passions, it was time to go and immerse myself in that part of France full of fascinating history. I did not want to be too deep inland and so began searching on internet for houses in medieval villages fairly close to the coast. That is when I found Eymet and even found a house that looked just right. But there was nothing I could do as I had not sold mine and had no idea when I would. The first thing was to get an estimate and then put it up for sale. The price the agent suggested was very encouraging, it would have covered all my expenses and had some left over. Again, to avoid adding a pointless commission on top, I advertised it myself and received a lot of enquiries, mostly from Brits. I have always told agents that I would probably advertise the property myself and offered to pay them a fee for the valuation. Most of them declined save a couple in the South. Things looked hopeful and after a couple of months, many enquiries and few visits, a young French couple came to see the house and loved it. They made an offer that was acceptable to me, again with some of the furniture and as they needed a mortgage it was not absolutely certain the sale would go through but they struck me as responsible and dependable types. I waited for their bank to confirm their mortgage in principle and then, in the winter of 2011, I set off for Eymet.

DORDOGNE IS NOT WHAT IT SEEMS

The Village that is more British than French

This time it was a renovated house I was seeking, or at least one that was immediately habitable. Emma, one of the local British estate agents, showed me a village house (the same house I had seen earlier and was delighted to find it was still for sale) that had been done up by the English owners and was for sale at more than it was worth but they told me Dordogne is an expensive area. It is now part of Nouvelle-Aquitaine, the largest administrative region in France with 12 Departments. It is well known that there is a large British community in Dordogne but what nobody told me was that in Eymet - the village I was now going to reside in - the population was at least 35% British in 2010. I did not mind the house being terraced, the only feature that left me dubious was the fact that it was right on the road. When I enquired if it was a busy road, the estate agent replied, 'not at all, it is just a quiet minor street.' 'How do you know, if you do not live here?' I asked. But she insisted that she was in Eymet quite often and every time she had shown the house she never saw any traffic. I gave her the benefit of the doubt but it stayed in my mind as a possible hazard for Mel who was used to be free and would have to put him on a lead before opening the front door.

The house had a small terraced garden on the south side and a balcony on the 1st floor. Before returning to Archingeay I instructed a local English DIY man to carry out a few works so it would be ready for me to move into. It is always a risk doing works in a house before one has bought it because if for any reason the sale falls through, it is the owners who enjoy the benefit of the improvements. Moreover, the owners can always say that they want the property to be put back to its original state and that can be even more disastrous but in this case they were cosmetic works like repainting and tidying up the terrace, and I intuitively trusted the vendors. Everything went smoothly with the sale of the house in Charente-Maritime and in January 2011, I moved to Dordogne. One thing that immediately pleased me was the number of good restaurants in the village, there was even a tea room and a pub. One of the restaurants was an excellent Pizzeria that was only opened from April to October and the owner, who was Italian, made so much money that he spent the winters in one of those desirable islands like the Caribbean or the Seychelles. I am no pizza expert but it was truly delicious.

I spent February and March furnishing the house and carrying out minor improvements. The kitchen was sizeable, the largest I have ever had in fact, apart from those in the Middle East or Hong Kong when I was living there but they were rentals. Suddenly there was so much working space I could really begin to cook in a serious way. (Wishful thinking!) The nearest town for shops was Bergerac and was only 20 minutes away on a very panoramic route. In the terraced garden there was a tiny loggia that I started using for painting large canvases. I painted watercolours in the kitchen on the large round table I bought in Eymet. Walking around the village with Mel (a dog is not just a great companion but it forces one to go out and walk and occasionally meet new people) I stumbled on a quaint shop with a notice in the window; '*rembourrage et empaillage de chaises anciennes*' and I went in to talk to the blonde French restorer of antique chairs who smiled at me and probably took me for a potential client. Her name was Isabelle. I discovered she was also a painter and I proposed to her that we do an exhibition together. She did not seem to think I was mad and was fairly open to the idea so I had a new project to work on. The medieval Chateau in Eymet had been built in the 13th century before the creation of the Bastide and was originally English but changed hands several times in the Middle Ages. It was now used as a museum and it was there that I intended to put up the exhibition. I was amazed that they agreed immediately and so Isabelle and I started preparing our work for the expo that was to take place in July. During that summer I also participated in a collective exhibition at the Chateau de Duras, a medieval castle on a hilltop in a village that is much loved by the English.

In the same street but three houses further along from me lived a wonderful French woman who spoke perfect English and she had an old female Labrador who got on well with Mel so we shared promenades together. Marie-Claire was a teacher; she taught English to French students and French to English students, as well as history, Latin and who knows what else. She was one of the few French people to invite me in her house whenever I wished. In front of her lived Charlotte, another single French woman; she rented the house from Marie-Claire's daughter who lived in UK. Charlotte also had a dog who luckily got on very well with Mel who, as a true French male subject, loves females but is very *parti pris* with males; he is small and like Napoleon, wishes to dominate them all, even after his testicles have been removed. Fortunately, the two dogs in my street were females and they both adored him.

Charlotte was an odd kind of person, according to Marie-Claire she suffered from a neurosis and was an aristocratic eccentric snob, which was an impressive statement coming from Marie-Claire who herself was of noble birth. The French are obsessed with the idea of nobility and equality. It is illogical for a nation that prides itself to be utterly logical. This paradox throws light on the explosiveness of its citizens and perhaps explains the reasons behind some historical events, like the Revolution. It could have something to do with the system of ranks; something everyone in France has - or should have. Nobody is without a *statut;* a waiter or a plumber have ranks; each profession, even the lowest, is part of a *corps de métiers* and enjoys certain concessions. Some of those concessions have nowadays been erased because of the economic revolution but as the French are not particularly moved by money or productivity, they still cling on to those few special rights that survive. The idea of personal freedom is ultimately connected to nobility whereas in England and America, for example, people are free if they and their property remain inviolable. (This validates the right to own firearms).

Charlotte could boldly go out in the mornings in pyjamas and slippers and walk her dog in the village whilst talking to herself because she was aristocratic and could therefore enjoy total personal freedom to do and be as she wished. I liked her, not only because she bought one of my paintings, but because she allowed others to enjoy the same liberty that she herself relished. She was writing a medical book by hand and was resolute in avoiding the use of computers or any technological gadgets because she believed they discharged harmful magnetic waves. So she relied on reference books borrowed from the library and the old encyclopaedias she owned. I told her she could come and do searches on my laptop but she declined the offer with the same fury one rejects an invitation to visit slaughterhouses. Charlotte and Marie-Claire came for tea a few times and complimented me on the way I decorated the house.

The exhibition was a success, especially for Isabelle who had a substantial invitation list, less for me who had just arrived but I was perfectly happy about everything and got some publicity too. Eymet in the summer is full of visitors, in particular on Thursdays which is the market day and is full of bright stalls with flowers, hand-made bags and clothes, food and the typical products of the region. English people meet up and then either go to the pub or one of the restaurants. It has been said that expats living in Dordogne are different; they are more snotty and cultured. My experience of them was not sufficiently vast to either confirm or deny this but it is certainly a region that attracts epicureans and in particular lovers of *foie gras* and other meat specialities as well as good wine. In any case it is a lovely region, albeit a bit damp in the winter. I was amazed at how much meat is produced and sold in Dordogne. Being a sort of vegetarian, it was disturbing to find slaughterhouses on the outskirts of every sizeable village. The meat sellers may not have solely existed for the purpose of feeding the locals but the locals were certainly butchering animals to feed outsiders.

If you walked in the streets of Eymet you were more likely to hear English being spoken than French but were the English happy or annoyed about that? My general perception was that some of them were perfectly delighted to live in France as if it were a mere British outpost whilst others wished to blend into the French culture and way of life thus regretted all the other Brits who walked the streets sunburned and slightly pissed. How could the French not be happy to have so many Brits living in their country? They boosted their economy and gave them something to talk about. If, despite the veneration they hold for their language, some French traders have finally given in to learning English, it is because it is the only way they can communicate and sell their products to the British who, with some significant exceptions, are quite happy to live in France without ever feeling the need to speak French.

Autumn was approaching and even if the house was comfortable and the village was charming, there was something missing. My sister told me I was like Juliette Binoche in the film '*Chocolat*,' when the north wind began to blow she had to pack her things and go somewhere else. I was only half way through my pilgrimages but at the time I did not know they would persist until the day I finally found a place that invited me to stay. Or I would find a project that would keep me still for a while, like writing a book about it all. Rural France, or '*La France Profonde*,' can be somewhat antagonistic and for someone like me who has a tendency to love solitude, it is even more alienating. It takes time to get to know people in those kinds of habitats and I am never in a place long enough for that to happen, even if I do my best to familiarise with the locals. There is more than one reason for my meanderings but I will come back to this later. So the autumn had arrived and the impulse to move somewhere different was getting stronger. I decided to put the house up for sale and by the end of 2011, I had already sold it and found another to buy.

This time my intuition directed me toward the south and specifically to Tarn & Garonne, a region yet unknown to me. Marie-Claire and Charlotte were sorry to see me leave but there was not anyone else I regretted leaving behind. It sounds as if I am a cold and cynical person; on the contrary, I have deep feelings and am extremely sensitive but I do not get attached to houses, locations, things, and to most people. A friend is a real treasure and though I admit I am not very good at bonding and working at relationships – in fact it is definitely one of my failings – whenever I have had the feeling someone could be a true friend, I invested everything in trying to merit that friendship. Acquaintances and 'short-lived friendships' have been and are numerous in my life but true friends do not appear often on the stage. I do not expect real friends to knock on my door and say, 'hey, I am a true friend!' Or to find them at the drop of a hat and without having contributed to creating a real bond. It takes a lot of affinity, tolerance and love. To be honest I am not absolutely sure true friends fit into a specific archetypal classification. They may cross our path and not be recognized or stay with us until they, or us, change, and then move on to find another more akin mate. I have been convinced so often that someone was a real friend and then for unexplained reasons ceased to be. It must have been something I had done; some deep regret or disillusionment that cause them to dump me. Would a true friend wish to talk it over, reveal the reason for the discontent or prefer disassociation and never see their friend again?

THE VILLAGE BETWEEN THREE DEPARTEMENTS

A Sacré Transformation

The next house was in a village called Puylagarde in Tarn & Garonne. Once more, it was advertised as 'habitable' but for me it was not and the roof in particular needed total renovation. I made an offer and found a local artisan who could do some preparatory work before I moved. I took a risk again but it enabled me to live in the house instead of renting for a while. All the houses I buy are modest and limited in budget, thus I have to be very intelligent in managing my finances, everything is calculated beforehand and though there may be occasional surprises - and there have certainly been - most of the time I am not far off the mark. Experience has taught me a lot about prices, materials and time required for every specific undertaking. It has not taught me enough about people though and being a person who trusts what someone says, all the times I unsuspectingly trusted and was taken in have not yet been able to change my basic character altogether. They have however helped me become wiser. The agent who sold me the next house, for example, told me the most evident lies with a poker face I could have slang a glass of cold water on but I kept silent and found solutions elsewhere. As the wayfaring journey continued I have learned to find my own solutions to problems. I was moving to another uncharted territory; same country but different region and though people are the same everywhere, it has become quite clear to me that each region encompasses subtle differences.

The first time I arrived in Puylagarde I knew I was not going to stay there for a long time. Why? It was just a feeling, an impression. Rural villages can be very unforthcoming and harsh, it depends on the type and number of foreigners living there. This is because if the locals relate with a variety of different people instead of always interacting with their own insular types (mainly farmers or small entrepreneurs) their perception changes and they are less parochial. As my journey progresses I will discover that, for some mysterious reason, in every place I move to, there is always a woman who stands against me; she is often spiteful and antagonistic. Sometimes she is married but for the most part she is single. I often tell myself to be more guarded and taciturn but my need to communicate is too strong, more so because I spend most of the time in solitude. I say *bonjour* to everyone and help someone if I can but whatever I do – or do not do – I seem to attract attention anyway. A foreign active, frank and seemingly fearless single woman who arrives out of nowhere in a village in rural France is inevitably open to cautious distrust and susceptible to criticism.

Once again, I moved into a new house in the middle of winter and having been empty for some time, the place was absolutely gelid. Luckily, I inherited a wood burner, all I had to do was find the wood. I met a man who worked for the Mairie – I always seek an artisan in the Mairie when I arrive in a new place because the *cantonnier* (roadmender) is invariably an honest and reliable person in addition to knowing everything and everyone in the village – and asked him where I could buy fire wood. He offered to deliver it and voilà I had found my guardian angel. He not only provided me with wood but he did various jobs whenever he had free time at very reasonable rates. The cantonnier is the *in loco* person who contributes to generate village economies. He is also a messenger, a broadcaster of gossip and village news.

The attic was insulated by the artisan I had engaged before moving and he also painted the interior. I usually do this myself but only if I move in warm weather and can leave the windows open. I lived on the first floor which was accessed by an external staircase. The ground floor had its own independent entrance and could be transformed into an apartment the same size as the first floor and idem for the attic; 60sqm each floor. It was one of my considerations when buying the property, that one day I could rent the ground floor and have an income but it was clearly not thought through. The house was detached, save for the southern side which was partly joined to another house, and that was one of the drawbacks. The *cantonnier* told me there had been a water problem on that joining wall and that it was the Mairie's responsibility to put it right. Basically, the neighbour's gutters were draining in my house's mains drainage and as long as nobody complained there was no need to fix the problem but when I arrived it became essential to rectify it in case I discovered it and protested. So, after a few weeks the Mairie sent workers to do what was necessary; they were fast and efficient and cleaned up all the mess without me having to ask them.

The winter was now coming to an end and the garden, which was north-facing, was beginning to get some sunlight and the last snow was slowly disappearing. The first thing to do was the roof and the façades of the house as they were in a bad state. I got various estimates (always advisable to get three quotes) and after giving the customary *acompte* (advance payment) the work on the façade started fairly soon and was shortly followed by the complete restoration of the roof.

The house now looked quite different, so much so that people used to stop in front and look at it with great curiosity. I guessed it had been left to itself for many years and the change was quite drastic. Luckily, the artisans who carried out these major works were really professional and even agreeable to have on site. I rebuilt the garden wall and done some preparatory work on the ground floor. It needed a new entrance door and internal insulation. The door was done fairly rapidly but had difficulty finding a *plaquiste* – a drywall expert. I looked up angloinfo, an expat site with all sorts of helpful contacts, and found a few Brits in the area. One arrived in a beautiful new Range Rover, dressed in a good quality suit. When I met him I thought there was a mistake somewhere in the contact so I asked him if he indeed came for an insulating job. He said yes, so I explained what was needed and asked him if he had done anything like that before. 'No,' he replied, 'but I am sure it's not that difficult and I can assure you it will be perfectly done.' I thanked him and said he would be contacted after some reflection, which was naturally a lie but did not wish to get into a quarrel with him. In the end I found a French artisan at double the price and perhaps at half the quality but the job got done. It is always tricky to find and engage new artisans when you do not know them. Most people do not like to recommend anyone because they do not want to be blamed in case of disappointments and so one has to rely on intuition and experience. The nuisance is that you can fall on someone who turns out to be not only incompetent but also irritable and touchy. In fact the latter is almost always the case with French artisans, whether they are good or not, they detest any form of criticism so you have to accept what they do, pay them and keep your mouth shut, which is a slight problem for me. And so I have made many enemies and undoubtedly will make more as time goes on. What really vexes me is the fact that they often try to rip me off and to make it worse they do so with an intolerably unpleasant attitude. Of all the difficulties and strain of moving and renovating so many times, this is the worst aspect and I have developed a mild aversion to artisans.

There was a woman in the village – Evelyne - who lived a few metres from me and seemed to display a particular friendly disposition toward me. This naturally pleased me and I tried to be graceful and amiable with her but I soon found out that she was seeking my participation in her pseudo-religious association that preached the Kabbalah and similar subjects. In our conversations, I spoke of my experience in an esoteric society, and when she realized I was not totally uninstructed on her pet subjects, she became cold and antagonistic. It was a pity she did not take advantage of the opportunity that presented itself to her and she did not understand that it was better to exchange rather than to impose. She was clearly frustrated and the more she tried to inflict her dogma on me and failed, the more embittered she became. Relations between us slackened somewhat until they became non-existent. This kind of thing has happened more than once to me. As when I meet someone the first time I give the impression of being meek and stupid because instead of imposing myself I tend to listen and ask questions aimed at giving me an idea about them – they often assume I am easily manipulated and they try to manoeuvre and impose their will on me. This infuriates me because I am far from being easily handled so it becomes necessary for me to either avoid them or defend myself which gives rise to friction and antipathy. They are disappointed because their plan failed and I am cheesed off because once again I have not been able to bring that kind of situation to the next level. Learning how to handle unintelligence is something that does not come easy. One of the things my father used to say was to never underestimate people and one can easily distinguish the level of a person's education by whether they undervalue others or not.

Unfortunately, my neighbour's daughter was on the war path with me and the reason was a mystery. She was at least 20 years younger, married, well-off and lived in a stunning house that her parents built for her and I never had one conversation with her. Why she ever felt animosity or jealousy toward me is beyond my imagination. But there it was. Her mother and father however became sort of friends to me, not immediately but after a while. He was a farmer and she, a retired nurse. It took me longer to gain their sympathy but in the end, we were sharing many conversations on hot summer afternoons under the shade of their floral terrace. There was a Dutch man in the village with whom I spoke every now and then; he boasted about being a resident there for 16 years as if it denoted a prized achievement. I could easily understand why he was proud of his record; the longer one stays in a French village, the more easily accepted and respected one is by the local people. No chance of that happening to me…

By the end of summer, I had nearly finished the ground floor and it could easily have been lived in or rented. It had its own entrance and terrace. The idea of renting it crossed my mind but did I want to stay in that village for any length of time? Puylagarde – known as *La Cité de Cheval* - and surrounding areas consists of farming and has nothing interesting to entice tourism. However, there are some attractions nearby; for example, the Lot is only a mile away and is indeed a lovely region, l'Aveyron with its beautiful villages like Najac is also easily reachable and the medieval Saint-Antonin-Noble-Val – another predominantly English village - is just over half hour drive. The Tarn department with the wonderful city of Albi is likewise accessible in less than one hour. It is an area I liked a lot, especially the Lot (no pun intended) but in order to stay I would have had to find new projects. The renovation of the house had once again nearly emptied my bank account and even if I rented the ground floor there was no guarantee it would have provided me with an adequate income.

After serious consideration, I decided to spend the winter there and put the house up for sale in the spring. Oddly enough time went by rather quickly and between finishing the downstairs and visiting the most interesting places in the surrounding areas spring arrived almost without warning. I discovered 7 Templar Commanderies in the Tarn & Garonne, some extremely well preserved and well worth a visit even if just for the architecture. As well as medieval architecture, one of my many interests is Knights Templars; their legends, history, purpose. I called the local agent for an estimate and put the house for sale in February 2012 and it took just over four months to find a purchaser. For three months there was nothing happening and I was beginning to worry, then all of a sudden there were two buyers who wanted the house with a passion and they both called from my personal advert. I wanted to sell it to the British people who were so appreciative of the work done rather than to the French woman who pointed out only what to her were negative points. Unfortunately, the British hesitated and in the meantime the woman made an offer conditional on a very snap decision on my part. She contacted the notary who unexpectedly reacted very fast and had the preliminary ready in a day. I had to say yes or no and as there had been so little feedback, I accepted the offer. Two days later the British couple called and offered me 5.000 euros more but I had already signed and was obliged to refuse with much regret. I felt I had been told to sign under duress, both from the woman and the notary who either had nothing to do - notaries are famous for being slow – or acted with bias in favour of the purchaser. Perhaps I did not like to admit that panic got the best of me and thus lost my cool. In any case I learned a lesson at a considerable cost; I was going to be very careful and avoid being manoeuvred or pressurized into making quick decisions.

You may be wondering how I could have bought and sold in such brief intervals without incurring capital gains taxes. The reason is that every house has been a '*résidence principale*' and I do not own any other property. The notary is obliged to put in the contract whether it is or not and though it has crossed my mind that one day they will catch up with me and be tempted to squeeze some money out of me, I already have a letter ready for them. The first question I will ask them is: 'have you not had enough money from me?' I have paid taxes and notaries every time I have bought a house; have given work to artisans, paid all my local taxes, improved a great number of run-down and shabby properties and reinvested whatever I gained in one property into the next one. My pension is not sufficient to live on and instead of claiming benefits from the

State, which I could do, I have struggled through thick and thin without ever giving up in order to keep my head above water. There are plenty of people in France who prefer to receive unemployment benefits and laze around rather than be creative and invent something to do. I have never asked the French State for anything. I have only given. My sister always says they should offer me a medal but then she is good-natured and credulous.

THE DIE IS CAST

The Cat that Sees Itself as a Tiger

The thrilling part was deciding where to move to next. One of the differences between Provence and other regions is that it is not quite so rural; it grows lavender, olives and vines and you will see the occasional horse but not livestock. The rustic and bucolic landscapes are fine but I missed the mountains, the fields of lavender, the vineyards and the light. The light. There is a reason why artists have wanted to live in Provence, there is nowhere else in France where the light is so radiant. The Mistral is a northern dry wind and because it is high, it clears the sky of all traces of humidity and dust and gives a bright clarity to the air thus making it a deep, dazzling blue colour. It comes down through the Bouches-du-Rhône and whereas in the winter it can be glacial, in the hot summers it is a godsend. It is a mighty wind and is also known by either the White, Black or Summer Mistral and they are all variations of the same wind. In Languedoc they have the Tramontane, also a northern cold wind but less dry than the Mistral; together with the Cers, a damp wind from the Atlantic, and the Marin, another damp wind from the sea, make the Languedoc – in particular the Aude department - the windiest French region.

Provence was the first region I encountered and loved; I missed most of all the luminosity and the fact that I could easily and rapidly drive to visit my sister in Italy. Strict regulations of chemical pesticides in the environment had been applied in Provence for some time now and since 1st January 2017, self-service sale of chemical pesticides is no longer permitted. These products are issued after a personalized advice given by a certified seller. After having witnessed how farmers treat the soil and breed the animals, I was longing for a landscape that had the colours of inspiration and the glow of creative vision. The only snag about Provence was that property is very expensive, it was even more so in 2011; since then prices have decreased somewhat. The only department where I could afford anything was Les Alpes-de-Haute-Provence or the hinterland villages in Alpes-Maritimes. Once again, I was yearning for some urbanity and culture. There are not many large towns in the Haute-Provence; the only one I knew was Digne-les-Bains and though it never thrilled me, it was nevertheless more than a village and less than a city. So my search was immediately directed there without wasting any time. I found the place that in many ways was ideal. It was a ground floor apartment in a period house with only four flats and it had a large terrace, a garden and a garage. It was situated in walking distance to the centre but far enough to avoid the noise and bustle. After Avignon, living in a city was out of the question but I was familiar with Digne and it does not fit into the category of noisy and crowded metropolis. In addition, the fact that there were only four flats, if I was lucky I would not encounter rowdy tenants.

The visit was done through an agent who passed on my offer to the owner - an Italian in Provence – and I never knew if my lower offer was accepted immediately because it was after all higher than they expected or because they were desperate to sell. My property hunts have mostly occurred in the autumn and before the winter vendors are generally more flexible about negotiating; they know the winter is long and properties deteriorate very quickly. The flat was very small (37sqm) with huge windows so it was extremely bright and the view was superb. The terrace was bigger than the apartment and for someone with money and building permission it would have been ideal if it was converted into living space by simply opening a door in the wall of the living room.

So around September 2012 I moved in and had to be very acrobatic and creative in order to fit my furniture into such a small space. Fortunately, the garage helped in accommodating the surplus. I had the kitchen redone but could not do anything in the tiny shower room. The flaws and drawbacks began to reveal themselves. The first and immediate one – though why I did not notice it when I visited the place puzzled me – was the railway line just behind the road outside the entrance of the property. Trains were not so frequent but they could be heard inside the flat with the windows shut. So could the traffic on the road. When I viewed the property, it was in July and even though I noticed a few cars, it did not strike me as a potential nuisance but then it was in the middle of the afternoon. In the rush hours traffic changed drastically not only for the noise but the pollution as well. I could smell the carbon monoxide and other exhaust fumes chemicals from my flat while I was having breakfast in the early morning. I tried to insulate the front door as much as possible but it did not help much.

Life in a town was a pleasant change from rurality and after arranging the flat as I wanted, I started an English conversation group. I had already done it once and it seemed to be appreciated; it was free and open to everyone who wanted to learn and practice the English language. In Digne the group grew very quickly to twelve members, mostly young students, and we met once a week for two hours. After a while I decided to ask them for one euro each, a symbolic amount obviously but the purpose of it was to discharge them of any sense of indebtedness toward me as well as exonerating them of any feeling of exploitation toward me. There were no travel expenses on my part because I walked to the multimedia library, where we met, but that was not the point. Humans rarely appreciate things that are freely given and if they do they do not always show it.

The apartment above me was rented by a single girl who was only there at weekends and spent most of the time in bed with her boyfriend but it was enough to make me realize that the insulation of the house was very poor indeed. It was an old building and it sounded as if the wooden floor of the apartment above and the plaster ceiling of my flat was all there was to separate the two. Since she was a tenant she could leave when she wanted with very little notice but what would happen if the next occupier/s lived there all the time; that was going to be a problem indeed. Without wishing to be foreboding, what I surmised would happen it actually did after two months. The flat was now occupied by a single mother with two very noisy children. Their living room was above my bedroom and between the stamping and the screaming I could not even hear my thoughts. I went to offer them a thick carpet which the mother accepted and asked her to put it on their living room floor to see if it would muffle the sound. It did help a bit but if I was obliged to take sleeping pills – I tried putting ear plugs but they made me feel as if I was constraining myself and did not like them – then that was a good reason for putting an end to the situation. Ergo, it was me who had to leave. They were certainly not going to as the business of moving a family is economically taxing and in any case, they had no reason to want to leave.

I knew the area fairly well from my previous habitations in Provence - Digne was only 45 minutes' drive from the first house I had bought in France – and there were places I love like Forcalquier, Moustière-Sainte-Marie and The Parc Naturel Régional du Verdon that is absolutely marvellous. Les Gorges-du-Verdon is an area with mountains and canyons with the emerald Verdon flowing through them that is of spectacular beauty; its nature is almost supernatural. When I visited the Canyon the first time with Michel I was extremely impressed and wondered why there was only the occasional car when on the Coast road you hardly moved at all in the congested traffic. Why such marvel was still relatively undiscovered was difficult to figure out but also a welcome surprise.

The motorway is close-by, there is a steam train that goes to Nice twice a day (Le Train des Pignes), there is a Spa just outside the town and

Digne is surrounded by no less than 7 Regional Parks thus making it one of the most protected natural areas in France. You might say that Digne – and its surrounding areas – is the genuine hard-core Provence. The town itself is rather dull, more administrative than picturesque, but well organised and functions like a Swiss clock.

I tried to keep myself busy and even found a dog training school close-by which I considered joining in an attempt to make Mel less mischievous. He was never taught to obey by anyone before me and when I rescued him he was already over a year old. It was expensive but I thought it was worth trying. Every Saturday morning off we went to join a bunch of other assorted dog races that Mel found absolutely exhilarating, being such a sociable creature. Mel seemed to understand immediately what he was there for and he started obeying orders in a fashion that left me quite speechless. Everyone congratulated me and asked me why I was there since he was so well-trained and obedient. I was furious and totally bewildered. The moment we left the school he immediately reverted back to his normal self; boisterous and wild. I terminated the course I paid for and learned a few things I did not know about dogs but on the whole, it was a waste of money. It is incredible that a small animal like Mel can be so sharp-witted and intelligent; he would put some humans to shame.

I was not in Digne very long, just six months. The flat could not be sold at much more than I paid for, though it now looked much more attractive and even if the condominium charges were reasonable, it had a large garage and a private terrace and a garden, it did not seem feasible to me to ask more than the original price. But I was proved wrong by the agent who came to give an estimate. It was indeed more than I expected so to test their credibility I gave it to them for sale and waited to see what happened. Agents sometimes overestimate a property in order to lure sellers into giving it to them exclusively. They were also in charge of the condominium charges so that simplified things for everyone. They only brought two people and the second one made an offer. It was slightly lower than the asking price but then the asking price was higher than I expected, so I accepted immediately. Perhaps I could finally get some sleep.

At this point some of you are beginning to presume there is something wrong with me. After all, you will say, there is no property that is perfect, so why leave one to find another that is also imperfect? You are right of course and I know it is almost impossible to find the perfect home, even if I could pay a huge amount of money. There are too many of us; we have unfortunately blemished our Planet and made our society an excessive muddle of regulations and inevitable delusions. Someone said to me that for anyone to move so often there must be some emotional imbalance somewhere. This reveals much about the person who said it. The fact is that only a balanced person can live through such a stressful activity without coming out crippled or devastated. And in any case, it is foolish to assume we are all the same, we have no idea what others are or can be like so it is useless to judge them based on our own ignorance. All our judgements, according to the wise Don Miguel Ruiz, are based on our collective illusions.

I will tell you why all the moves for I do know the reason why I do something. The main one is that it is not possible to live in France on a pension such as mine, even economizing and scrimping all you want. Therefore, even though with every purchase I pay taxes and notaries, I try to make a little profit to help me pay the bills. The essential thing is to find myself after twelve years with the same amount of money as when I started and this has been my way of doing it. Another reason is that I enjoy transforming things; in this case houses. In another life, I have transformed vases into table lamps, wooden planks into libraries, fabrics into clothes and bedcovers and many other things. There is a huge amount of pleasure in looking at what I have done; seeing the improvement – sometimes the total change – of something that had no value and is now an exquisite thing. (We all have our perversions and this is one of mine). Another reason is that, putting aside what I just said, there has not been a place yet that has made my leaving more painful than my staying.

There is a spot I often visited not far from Digne – just under 50kms – that is wonderful for more than one reason. It is the Benedictine monastery Ganagobie. It sits on a plateau that was formed 20 to 25 million years ago at an altitude of 650metres overlooking the expanse of Forcalquier that was at that age covered by the sea. The place was apparently inhabited around 2000 BC and monastery life seems to date to the 10th century. There is an ancient mosaic that has been masterly restored. Apart from the Abbey, there are other elements that make it worth a visit. The vegetation on the plateau is very varied and rich; the views on the Durance valley are spectacular, there are some natural water springs and if one wants to stay it is possible to book a room in the monastery and enjoy the total peace and quiet of monastic life as well as listen to the Gregorian chants and sample the products from the monks' gardens. In the same area, there is the village Moustiers-Sainte-Marie that dates to the 5th Century and was built on the rocks with a bridge in the centre overlooking the river Riou. According to folklore an Italian potter stopped by in the Middle Ages and taught someone in the village how to make perfect milk white enamels and since then Moustiers has been famous for its faience and the golden star that a crusader returning from the Holy Land had strung between two cliffs. Descending from the village there is the picturesque Lac Sainte-Croix-du-Verdon, the third largest lake in France.

Moustiers-Sainte-Marie

Lac Sainte-Croix-du-Verdon

Despite not having done a major renovation in my Digne apartment, I was still fairly tired from the previous house so it would have suited me to find a place that needed very little work, that was in the environs and a house rather than a flat. There was not much hope of finding anything with a garden, garage or terrace as they are all in great demand in Provence and therefore highly priced. I had a shufti on internet and eventually found a small terraced house in a village called Puimichel which is further south and even closer to Ganagobie and Manosque; a town double the size of Digne and much more stimulating. The day the agent showed it to me it was so windy I could hardly stand up straight. I then discovered Puimichel is at 700m altitude. Being a hilltop village, the views were so amazing it did not occur to me that walking up and down the hills was going to put my painful knees to the test.

Whilst the selling process was going through I started packing some of my belongings; things I did not need in the interim like books, dvds, objects. I also put an advert in leboncoin.fr (a free site for buying and selling almost anything) for some objects that were stored in the garage. leboncoin is a very useful site; it has successfully sold my houses, car and objects. The new house had a cellar but there was no point in storing things I did not need. Through the years, and with so many removal, I reduced my belongings to the essentials, partly because my attitude toward possessions has changed drastically and because I have become weary of packing and unpacking the same things all the time. True, I have sold many pieces of furniture with the houses but what I mostly needed to reduce was the number of books (I have since got a kindle) which I regularly donated to the local libraries, the objects and clothes that I still had from when I worked. Some of the clothes I had already donated to the Red Cross and before leaving Digne I decided to condense my total wardrobe to the indispensable minimum that would fit into a child's closet. So, I filled the car with all the nice dresses, jackets, coats, shoes and sweaters that were still in my possession and delivered them to an association that catered for the needy.

It felt very good to do that; it made me feel lighter and freer.

I was thrilled about leaving Digne and above all to be able to remain in the same area. After my first visit with the agent, I chose a less windy day and went up to Puimichel a second time to acquaint myself with the road and the environs. It was obvious that there was no passing traffic; the only cars in the village belonged to the locals. There was no noise and no pollution, save that which the wind could bring from below but what it brought it could also take away. The road is very winding and panoramic and the beautiful landscape stopped me in my tracks more than once. It was a clear, sunny day, I could see the provençal Alpes in the distance and it was not even the highest point of the steep hill.

Col de Puimichel

   One aspect of moving that can be distressing is
the choice of a removal company. They can be
helpful and sympathetic but they can also be
incompetent and disagreeable. In all my moves in
France, there has not been one that equals those
in the Far East. They worked in silence, never
complained and delivered on time. There is one
thing about French workers – not just removers
but all artisans – that is puzzling and at the same
time infuriating - when they work, the whole
world has to stop for them as if their clients are at
their complete disposal and in their service. If a
carpenter, for example, comes to carry out a job

in the kitchen, everything has to be made easy and comfy for him; no clutter around where he has to work, no dogs to bother him, no demands put on him. He comes to do the job you asked and that is it, if you do not like it you can stuff it. The same for the removal people; they want to find everything perfectly packed, organised, the access to your house facilitated and no tantrums because it is they who are having a hard time, not you. They do not want to know that you have nearly done your back in trying to pack everything (for the second time that year) or that you have not slept, that you cannot give them unconditional attention because you have other things to attend to. And above all do not say the previous removers broke something because they will take it personally, tell you it was your fault because you were a lousy packer and in any case it will only antagonise them. So, you quietly swallow a sedative and repeat to yourself 'la vie est belle.'

ON THE LAVENDER ROUTE

A Room with a View

The first thing to do was to get an estimate for the painting before I moved in, obviously after checking that the vendors had no objection to this. If the house is empty the sellers never take exceptions to improvements being made (subject to knowing what they are and in any case never structural modifications) knowing full well that if the sale does not go through, they find themselves with an upgraded property free of charge. The only person who objects is the notary and this is because they wish to avoid contentions. I found a DIY French man via the Mairie and told him what needed doing. He demanded a sum that was excessive, wanted to be paid in cash and insisted on a down payment of 40%. I could not tell him to go to hell – though I wanted to – because I could not find anyone else and because once moved in, it is a mess to paint the ceilings and walls with all the furniture and objects in the way, especially in small spaces. So with much reluctance I told him to go ahead. The electricity needed upgrading too and I asked the artisan if he knew an electrician. 'Yes,' he replied, 'do not worry, I take care of everything.' This cheesed me off somewhat for I knew what was coming. I told him it was an estimate I wanted and not to be taken care of so a few days later he sent me an electrician's quote for rewiring. At that price one could have rewired the whole village so I said thank you but no. He painted the house and other bits and pieces at breakneck speed and of course it was very poorly done. In fact, it was so unsatisfactory that I could not bring myself to pay him what he had demanded. Instead I paid what seemed correct for the job (having already given him nearly half in cash) and he reacted aggressively. This put a gloomy note on the project, a detestable déjà vu for me. Worst still, it stained the Mairie's reputation that up to that moment had been almost flawless.

Eventually I found a young electrician who did the rewiring at less than a quarter of the swindler's quote and did an impeccable job. I was already living in the house while he was working and by the end of May 2013, I had personally repainted the shutters, done a bit of cosmetic work on the two façades, repainted the front door and revamped the cellar. The terraced house was modest and small and could not be transformed into something else but it now looked more appreciable and charming.

When you move to a new place, the neighbours are inevitably curious about you. They want to identify who you are, where you come from, what you do and why you are there.

Quite a lot to deduce. Suspicion is something that is engraved in people's subconscious, it goes back to a primitive age when humans lived in small isolated communities and were fearful and diffident of outsiders. The neighbours in Puimichel were very eclectic. The middle-aged couple next door on my right, were from the North and, judging by their intimacy, had clearly met later in life. There was nobody living on my left but further along the road there was a single man who was an expert in herbs and wild plants and further still there lived a distinguished pianist. The terraced houses in my street, were built on the near summit of the village which meant that one had to either descend or go further uphill. The cellar was behind, on the southern façade of the house, and not there being an internal passage, it was necessary to walk up and down the steep slope every time something had to come up or go to the cellar. Luckily it never snowed in that area but it still required much strenuous effort. On the village street below the cave, there were two very friendly people who used the house as a holiday home.

They were from Paris and we sorted of bonded almost immediately. When summer came they always invited me on their vine-shaded terrace where, together with their usual hangers-on, we would spend time laughing, drinking and chatting.

Everyone I met told me there was a famous artist living in the village; she was called Arlette and when I finally met her and saw her work, I could confirm she was indeed a remarkable artist and the fact that she also had a number of dogs made her immediately empathic to me.

More significantly the village is the home of an astronomical observatory with the largest amateur telescope in the world (at the time: 102 cm). It was installed by Dany, a Belgian astronomer who, I later discovered, was married to Arlette the artist, but they lived separately. Being fascinated by astronomy, it did not take me long to visit the observatory and admire the sky at night. The views from Puimichel are really stunning, in particular from the area where the observatory is located, which is the highest point and the sky is of a limpidness rarely seen. As I suffered mild osteoarthritis in the knees, living nearly on top of a hill meant that if I wanted to go anywhere it was inevitable to either ascend or descend and the movement of bending knees was what caused me pain. However, any amount of pain was alleviated by the pleasure and joy of looking at the beauty all around me. In particular, during June and July, the overlapping lavender fields are a truly delightful sight.

Once I settled in – it did not take me long! – I went to the Mairie and enquired about exhibitions. They offered me the Council Hall and though I would have preferred to be part of a collective exhibition (thereby avoiding attracting all attention to me) it was impossible to find people to join me so I accepted whilst intuitively knowing it was a mistake. In a village where Arlette reigned – a much more polished artist than myself – how could I possibly hope to gain any acclaim or anything other than indifference. It was too late when I fully realized my intuition was right but it was pleasing to see that Arlette supported me. It is arrogant on my part to expect any praise for my artwork when I dedicate so little time to it. In reality – and perhaps unfortunately – I only have time to paint when there is a gap in my other activity, which is moving and renovating. It is a relaxing occupation and one that has accompanied me for so long I forget when it began. It is erratic and have been known to produce some good paintings and even sell them but it depends on the inspiration, the place where I live, the overriding feeling of the moment.

Of all the villages I have known so far, Puimichel is the one where I found the most eclectic and interesting people. Partly because most of them came from other places and partly because the village and its surroundings are so charming – it may seem strange but I am convinced that if people live in a peaceful and pleasant environment, they also become peaceful and pleasant, were they not so before. The other thing is that many charismatic persons have chosen to live in the South because of the quiet life and the sun. The French, some North Europeans and Americans tend to favour Provence whereas the British and Irish prefer the south-west like the Languedoc or Aquitaine. Provence has been a tourist attraction for much longer than Languedoc and has a certain sheen and extreme splendour that the South-West lacks; it has been the destination of the rich and famous from the early 19th century. The lack of heavy industries and the presence of art and crafts make it a region of subtle sensuality and fragrances. The hill-topped villages may be perched because of defence rather than ornament but they are still

arrestingly handsome. Whether it is the Luberon,
the Haut-Var, the Camargue or the Alps, (I
except the Côte d'Azur as it is almost a region
apart) Provence has incredibly varied and rugged
sceneries with some extremely vertiginous views.

  Looking through my photos collection, it is
easy to see which places have had the most
impact on my senses because it is where the
largest number of photos have been taken.
Puimichel is one of them. Not only have I
captured the sceneries many times because I was
moved by the colours and the charm but also of
myself because I must have felt more attractive.
It is true that the lily grows in a swamp but it is
also true that one is more likely to feel lovelier in
a luminous scene than in a dark and dismal
ambience. It is curious that the desire to
photograph myself has always taken place in a
peaceful village, where nature is at its best and,
above all, the views are wonderful. As you may
have concluded by now, staying in one place a
long time is not my penchant; however, there is
one place that can claim to have entrapped me

and that is Florence. The reason is exactly because of the view. I lived in a converted attic of an ancient villa on the southern hills overlooking Florence. From my terrace there was a view that arrested anyone's attention. The place was small, the ceiling way too low (my head was bruised all the time and I am not tall) the stairs were tiresome and the neighbour definitely nutty but the view was undisputably unique. I lived there for more years than I can brazenly admit.

We all have a month, or months, that we dislike; for me it is August. It is during this month that the majority of my properties have been put up for sale – unless I was already moving! It was the case of Puimchel. Summer was coming to an end, the people who became more than acquaintances were beginning to pack their bags and there was no project on the horizon that could keep me enthralled. The enchanting walks on the hills and the beautiful views were stored in my heart and my imagination; they are as fresh today as the first day I left. That was one of the years when I moved twice. Looking back, it seems incredible that I was there only five months, it ought to have been much longer. The main reason why things take on a vertiginous speed is that the sales of my houses take place surprisingly fast. I had put the Puimichel property up for sale at the end of August and by the end of October I was already in the new home. People have often remarked that they found a 'good atmosphere' in the places I inhabited - even if just for a few months. Up to the present day, I have kept in touch with all the purchasers of my properties; some have become friends, none of them have ever voiced any complaints. One of the reasons they sell quickly is that the price is correct. The other is that they are bright and truly habitable; but above all they are clean. It is surprising how many filthy houses I visited, it made me wonder how they could show photos of properties on internet with knickers on the dining table, unmade beds and rubbish on the floors. In fact when people came to visit, they often inadvertently commented on the cleanliness of the house, as if it was a special feature like a wood burner that loads itself up.

A WARRIOR MONK ON THE MOVE

To Find It, You Have to Know It Is There

The buyer of my house was in a kind of hurry so the sale procedure was carried out at a breakneck speed. This meant there was not much time for me to find a new home and it had to be found in the same department as long road trips were out of the question. Renting something was an alternative but in order to be accepted you have to show your monthly income is at least twice the amount of the rental and it was not my case. So, it was necessary to find a place that was reasonably priced, essentially habitable and, hopefully, with a view. When you have been used to some height with unimpeded fantastic panorama, it is not easy to accept looking at a stonewall. For those reasons I directed my search on the mountains towards the east and voilà I found a place in La Rochette at under two and half hours' drive across the mountains. It was advertised by the owner who told a lot of lies, as it later transpired. The pressure to find something and the limited time at my disposal were working against me but there were not many choices available.

On first impression it seemed an abandoned village, a place where one goes to get away from everything and be forgotten; it is certainly away from the madding crowds. The road to it is very winding and narrow and if you are by chance inspired to look at the spectacular views whilst driving, a glance at the precipices rapidly convinced you to give it up. The village is built on a rocky mountain so having spent hours getting there on circuitous roads, you now have to walk up and down mazy stairs between houses, bridges and tunnels.

The property was a portion of a large house, with its own private entrance but still it was not a house as advertised by the owner. It was indeed habitable but it did not have a convertible attic space as advertised. That was going to be vital for storing my personal effects that would not fit in the three-rooms apartment. Access to the attic was possible only via a ladder, which the owner conveniently declared was not available, and therefore it was only after I had bought the place that the attic revealed itself to be a mere plunder room; a small space under the eaves. I still managed to have boxes and other things stored there which in time got completely spoiled due to the leakages in the roof. Naturally, the owner claimed the roof had been redone and was in a perfect state.

The apartment was on the first and top floor of the old bâtisse, the portion below me was lived in – only half of the year – by a French couple who proved to be exquisitely charming and helpful. They were from Grasse but their family was originally from La Rochette. They knew everything about the village, its history and its people; the latter being basically five families and their respective descendants. The old folks still lived in the village all year round and the rest only went up in the summer months. So, in reality, most of the year I was going to share the village with a couple of senile gramps and three less senile but definitely doddery individuals. The one thing that was true among the lies in the advert, was the view, it was indeed glorious. Looking out of the window made me feel dizzy and awestruck.

Once again I moved into a new home in late autumn and winter was setting in. It was 2012. November, being usually a wet and dreary month, was not so at La Rochette. The days were full of sun with the occasional Mistral that had not yet picked up speed and ice. The heating had to be turned on at night as the temperature could descend considerably and the apartment had not been lived in all the time. The department is the Alpes-Maritimes so even though it is cooler at the 890 m altitude, it enjoys the same cloudless climate as Nice; the notoriously sought-after winter haven. The Côte d'Azur has its advantages but it does not have the unpolluted air and silence of La Rochette. You will say that everywhere is polluted nowadays and perhaps it is so but if you lived in La Rochette you would have noticed the difference every time you went down to the Coast. The number of cars is exorbitant, the noise is disturbing and the quality of the the air is poor; it would be much worse if it was not for the Mistral every now and then that blows away the impurities. Where are they blown to?

The removal men were outraged when they arrived and had to carry everything by hand. I was not happy either but there it was. I made a few improvements (the fireplace had to be removed because it took up space that was otherwise indispensable for the cooker) and settled in fairly rapidly.

The stairs were worrying me as my knees were not improving with age and Mel had to be taken out four times a day. He was left free to roam in the village, it is completely safe because there are no traffic dangers; there is only one road and that is at the top of the village and you can count on one hand the number of cars per day. Mel would have liked to meet some pals but there were none, save for the hunting dogs which were kept in an enclosed structure up the mountain. So when I went down to Nice I would often take him with me so he could meet other dogs and there were certainly a great number, especially little breeds who, unlike Mel, behaved impeccably walking beside their smartly dressed masters.

The problem of the missing space in the non-existent attic was resolved by my kind neighbour who lent me one of his cellars. This was not underground but on one of the village alleys in full sunlight all day. La Rochette means 'little rock' and in effect the village had been carved from the rocks. Quite a feat in those days when there were only donkeys and carts to help masons; in reality those villages were built for donkeys and carts and not vehicles, the lanes are much too narrow and some bridges are barely high enough for bicycle riders to pass under.

There are many perched villages in the hinterland and just above the Côte d'Azur, mostly in strategic locations as they needed to protect themselves from invaders. Some of these villages have acquired fame and attracted notable artists and celebrities, like Eze, Saint-Paul de Vence and Biot. La Rochette is a poor cousin in comparison but the difference is that you can leave the door to your house and your car open without fearing they will be broken into. There are no amenities and the road twists and turns but when you arrive you are welcomed by the kind of peace and beauty you do not find so easily elsewhere in the South of France.

The first winter passed by without unexpected surprises except for the snow that fell in February. After two nights and a full day, it measured more than 2 feet and though the road was promptly cleared, the village alleys were left to the residents to sort out. Each occupant had to clean his or her access to the house, that exercise was enough to warm anyone up. There were only five of us living there during the winter but with some elbow grease we managed to clear the snow. Fortunately the pavements had been done in an anti-slippery covering and ramps were fixed on all the walls, otherwise it would have been disastrous. Because of its isolated position, the village had no internet coverage so I was obliged to get it via satellite. The dish had been installed on the roof and could not be reached for removing the thick layer of snow that blocked the reception of the signal so I was without any means of communication for nearly a week. It was magic in a way and the fact of being cut off from everything did not worry me in the least. Mel found the whole experience exciting though the first day he got completely buried by the snow.

Spring 2013 was on the way and in March the first vipers began to introduce themselves to me. That is when they give birth and sometimes a litter can consist of 35 baby vipers. The first one happened to be in the little alley near my house and it was so small and short I assumed it was a new-born, the head was triangular and as I watched it move very slowly, it became apparent it was a viper. If it was young then there must be others all over the place, I said to myself, and that was un unsettling thought. The fact that I nearly put my foot on one did worry me a bit, not so much for me but for Mel who had the habit of cleaning floors everywhere and a bite from that viper (called *vipère d'Orsini*) could be lethal. It was a new challenge and one that caused me to make some research. A viper (or adder) never attacks and will only bite – they can give a 'dry bite,' which is without venom, or bite with venom – to defend itself, like when it is trodden on or, for example, they are provoked by a dog. The people in the village killed them but I preferred to either avoid them or create vibrations with my shoes or walking stick, in the hope they would sneak away. Vipers have excellent vision and infra-red auditory sense but as far as I know they do not hear you coming in soft shoes, that is why dogs are at risk. Having heard from an old man in the village that he had found one in his home, I became more vigilant and observant. As they are greysh in colour, they sort of blend in with the pavements and it is so easy not to notice them. I made a walking stick out of a boxwood branch and from that moment it has become my companion every time I go out. That spring I spent more time with my eyes fixed to the floor than to anything else and if I ever suffered from herpetophobia, then La Rochette cured me which goes to show that to conquer a fear it is better to immerse oneself in what causes it rather than avoid it.

Spring was stunningly beautiful but also surprisingly dangerous on those mountains. It was not just the vipers that turned a simple promenade into a prospective hazard. Being an area devoid of chemical pesticides, nature was full of potentially noxious creatures. Between the flees, the ticks, the spiders, the scorpions and the wasps, it felt like a battlefield sometimes. Mel developed an irritation caused by an aggression of flees despite the fact that he was treated monthly against ticks and flees. I felt sorry for the little darling for he had to be virtually covered with Frontline in order to deter the little bleeders. I spent the nights scratching myself and the days covering my arms and legs – at first with lavender oil but soon realised it was ineffective - with a strong anti-insect remedy.

One French habit I have come across is that they often use desherbant around their houses or in villages, that is why grass looks as if it has been burned. It may have been this or something else but during the summer Mel started vomiting and drinking a lot. He would not eat at all and after three days of this I was convinced it was a serious matter. So I looked for a vet but being the weekend, all I found was an emergency clinique in Nice that was open all the time. On Sunday morning I put Mel in the car and raced down to the clinique. He was X-rayed, thoroughly tested and examined and the vet concluded that there was no proof of contamination or poisoning. In effect they could not determine what caused his gastritis and that was not helpful at all for if there was something that had to be avoided, I did not know what it was. After treating Mel for a couple of days, he began to eat again and that was a good sign. The whole incident amounted to an incredible 450 euros and I promised myself to avoid the weekend emergency visits in the future.

Summer was in in full swing and the village was suddenly animated with people who came up from the Coast in search of fresh air and silent nights. I painted some watercolours and received two commissions, one of which was from the Mairie asking me to paint the village. I was thanked and paid for my watercolour of the village which now hangs in their Mairie's office. The other commission – a portrait - was also successfully delivered. It is a small thing but considering my career had been mainly in journalism and not art, it was rewarding to be recognised as a painter.

The apartment was comfortable enough but there was something missing; a terrace or a balcony. As I thought about it more and more, it became compelling to get a quote for creating one. Whenever I need an artisan it has always been my choice to use local people as much as possible. So I contacted two companies from nearby villages – no artisan existed in La Rochette – and received their estimate after a short while. In the meantime I asked the Mairie for the authorisation of the work. It was not possible to build a concrete terrace on the façade of the house and even if it had, the cost would have been enormous. As the bâtisse's foundations were built on the rocks below, the south-facing façade – which is where the balcony would be erected – was extremely high so that where I lived, that was only the first and last floor, gave the impression of being much higher when looked at from the lowest point. Therefore erecting the scaffolding would be the hardest and possibly the most expensive part of the project.

  The second winter was approaching and the need to find a project and make myself useful was pressing. Real estate prices were going down even on the Côte d'Azur so the chances of selling my apartment were very slim. The purchase had been a mistake, of that I was now persuaded, and I paid far too much for it. That too was a conviction and one that bothered me immensely. They say that you make a winning not on the sale of something but on the purchase. I knew it was slightly over the correct price when I bought it but when I discovered the missing attic and all the other flaws, it soon became apparent that this was going to be a losing venture. With the market as it was – and getting worse by the minute – it would never resell at the initial price; the only solution was to erect a balcony. Besides, it was primarily for my benefit; what a difference it would make to be able to sit outside and admire that breath-taking view. After all, even if it may take years to sell, it would not be so bad if I could admire that splendour by day and watch the sky by night from my own terrace.

I heavily ruminated on what could occupy my time in a place like La Rochette during the coming winter. Naturally if I was willing to drive down to the Coast I would have found things to do but it was an unlikely solution. The thought of teaching english crossed my mind so I signed up for a TEFL (Teaching English as a Foreign Language) course online and after three months'studies and exams, I was in possession of a teaching certificate that might or might not prove useful in the future. I joined a choir group in the neighbouring village (I must have been fairly desperate as I cannot sing at all) and the organiser, who was also teaching children in an elementary school in a large village toward the Coast, proposed that I teach them english. I immediately accepted because even if it was only twice a week, it would provide me with a project for which I needed to prepare. It was going to be on a voluntary basis but they would pay all my expenses which was good enough for me.

Not having ever taught children – in fact my experience with children in any form was very scarce – it was going to be a challenge. And indeed it was. They were toddlers (the older was 10 years old – and even though at the beginning learning English may have seemed a novelty to them, they quickly got bored and bothered so it was essential to find an amusing and distracting way of getting them to learn some words of a new language. So I designed flash cards, proposed games and created schemes that got them sufficiently interested to learn some English. In the middle of winter some of them got the flu and the class was suddenly much reduced. I must have caught some germs because a terrible bronchitis forced me to bed. The antibiotics I was given were clearly not fulfilling their purpose as it got worse and was obliged to take stronger medicines to avoid it turning into pneumonia. Taking Mel out for walks was a problem and it certainly contributed in me not recovering but there was nobody I could ask for help in the village. I have never been seriously sick, except the occasional cold and that was the first bronchitis I experienced - hopefully the last one. It did improve but I gave up teaching, not for fear of catching some other desease but because I believed the children were too young; their school syllabus was already fairly demanding and by the time it was English class, they had exhausted their learning and concentrating capacity. In short I believed it was a waste of time for all concerned. My resignation was accepted and it was not long after that works on the balcony started.

I had designed the wooden balcony and *comme d'habitude*, I asked for three quotes. Naturally I chose the least expensive. It belonged to a Tunisian builder who worked with his brother and imported labourers from his country whenever the need arose. Obviously he was registered at the Chambre de Métiers and could provide guarantees for his work. The other two quotes were from local French artisans. The fact that one of them proposed to use mélèze (larch) instead of sapin (fir) did not justify the high price. Larch is a coniferous tree just like the fir but it grows more slowly and, contrary to firs, looses its needles in autumn. It is regarded as the king of the forest and it is a beautiful and resistant wood to use. However, as the fir was much more inexpensive and I was assured by the builder that it was the perfect choice for that type of balcony, my decision was rapidly taken.

The construction of the balcony took more than a couple of weeks to be completed and the result was amazing. I could walk out of the french door of the bedroom in the morning and it was like as if I was suspended on a magic platform in the sky and welcomed into a pure marvel. It had been a good investment and though I knew I would not get my money back, it was simply wonderful to enjoy it whilst I was there, even for a day. The locals were very enthusiastic as they stared with their eyes up to the sky and told me it had been well done.

Mel was afraid to walk onto the balcony at first, he would put one paw through the door and then quickly go back inside. To tell the truth it did not feel quite safe to me either, it was an odd feeling to be standing so high and see the space below between the wooden boards. They had to leave a gap between the boards so that the rain would drain through but it did cause my heart to jump every time I put my foot outside. The balustrade was also a cause for apprehension; it seemed too fragile to support someone leaning on it who, unlike me, was heavy built. I waited a few months to see if it was just my impression but it wobbled every time I touched it so it had to be reinforced. After this was done, it really changed everything.

It was now 2015 and I had been in that place for nearly two years, the longest period ever in France. It was time to put the apartment up for sale. Even without asking an agent, I already had an idea of the price it could be sold for. I was going to lose at least 25.000 euros which on a small budget, is a considerable loss. The market gave no sign of improvement, on the contrary it indicated a long-term stagnation; even today –

2017 – it has not recovered yet. So, I had to put a cross on it, as the saying goes, and resign myself to go before it might get worse. In a way, it seemed an irony that of all places I would lose money in Provence where real estate investments have always been unfailing. I called an estate agent from Nice and when he eventually came, he confirmed my own estimation. He said it would have been better to give him exclusivity and I agreed to do that for three months. The fact of exclusivity has never been a convincing issue to me, probably because I am so accustomed to be independent and not rely on other people to come up with results. That, however, was a different situation; besides, it was improbable he would have even thought about my place twice had I not given him the exclusive selling right. Spring went by, another summer made its entry and the south-facing balcony was getting positively hot. It was wonderful to have breakfast there in the morning and watch the sky after dark but could not stand the heat during the day.

Higher up the mountain, but still in the municipality of La Rochette, there is a Zen Sôtô

Buddhist monastery – Ei Tai Ji – that provides meditation retreats and teachings. The road up the mountain is either done on foot or with a 4-wheel drive as it is very steep and rugged. The view from that position is even more impressive. One of the monks who reside there goes down to Nice Airport with a pick-up truck to fetch people who come for a retreat or collects them from the village parking lot when they arrive with their own cars. The total silence that I found sublime in La Rochette was even more complete up at the monastery; every now and then one could hear the sound of hanging bells. One of the monks has become the village road sweeper. He plays the guitar like Segovia and speaks at least five different languages. It was an unusual kind of experience to be greeted with a bow and folded hands in a setting where the only humans were old provençal blokes who liked hunting wild boars.

Three months had passed and no news from the agent. He said it was very difficult to find someone who would drive all the way up there. His exclusivity had ended so I took the matter in my hands. As usual I advertised in *leboncoin* in French and on another site in English and then waited. In the meantime, I wrote a couple of articles for The Riviera Times and then started writing an erotic book. Why an erotic book? It all started when I had that terrible bronchitis in the winter and had visited the doctor in a large village in the valley below. She wore a shirt that was nearly unbuttoned to her waist, black leather boots and tight jeans; she had long blond hair and sharp blue eyes. Not at all the typical doctor one expects to find, even for someone so broadminded and flexible as myself. When I asked her if she accepted new patients she said '*non*!' and added that she preferred men in general. I have no idea why but when I got back, the idea of writing an erotic novel with her as heroine got hold of me quite unexpectedly. My imagination ran wild with visions of her *salle d'attente* full of men waiting for their turn. Perhaps it was the shock that awoke some latent sensual instinct or touched an erogenous part deep in me. The novel is half written to this day and I blush every time I read what I have written and ask myself where such exciting stuff could possibly come from. It will never be completed and will probably end up in the rubbish bin one day in the future.

Spring was followed by another summer; there were less vipers around that second year though the other venomous creatures had not diminished but I was stung much less. Perhaps I was getting used to them or them to me. During the summer I had two friends come to stay and they enjoyed the balcony a great deal; they left rather sunburned but very relaxed. I shared a few lunches with Michel who lived on the parallel mountain across the valley. My French advert generated very few enquiries as when they looked up the location on Google they evidently decided it was too far from anywhere. Only one person actually drove up from Nice to visit the property; he was very interested and made me an offer that I refused because it was too low and believed I could sell it at the asking price, that was already low enough. I later regretted not having accepted it but perhaps I was lacking faith in that exact moment. From the English ad I received a call from a Japanese artist who lived in London and longed to be in a quiet place on the hills where she could paint her trendy canvases. After some long telephone discussions, she decided to fly to Nice and come to visit my place. She was thrilled and inspired by the views but called the next day to say that it was too isolated and she would not feel at ease there on her own. She had fallen in love with my photos and not with the actual location.

My hopes were beginning to fade and did not know what to do. I started practising meditation every day for one hour and focussed on being positive. One cold winter day I received an enquiry by a Russian that originated from *leboncoin*. I deduced it was a scam so I deleted it and forgot about it. Then it arrived a second time a few days later with the addendum 'I am genuinely interested in your property, please reply,' written in the type of French one has automatically translated online. I sent a few more photos and a few extra bits of information and the Russian man said he wanted to come and visit. He said he would fly out for the day the next week, as it happened just the week when the weather forecast was estimated to be the worst. Having sent him a selection of photos with brilliant blue skies and told him that the area enjoyed the best sunny climate even in winter, it was going to be a huge let-down but despite my suggestion to postpone his trip, he nevertheless came. So, on the ghastliest February day with rain, hail, snow and visibility zero, he knocked on my door at exactly the time he planned to arrive. I was totally astonished that he had driven up the road I knew so well to be risky on the best of days, let alone on slippery and frosty ground. The splendid views were nowhere to be seen and all I could do was apologise and offer him some coffee. He said if he liked it on a day like that, he could only adore it on a sunny day. He took copious photos and left saying he would contact me the next day with his decision. I always trust my intuition but in that instance I was so dubious nothing could convince me he would contact me again.

The next day I received an email saying he and his wife loved my place and wanted to buy it at the asking price. It was such a surreal moment for me I cannot describe it. I thought perhaps it was a miracle because rationally it was difficult to accept. A Russian living in UK who reads an advert on a French site (that is primarily intended for the French market) and buys a place that even locals cannot picture themselves living in. It is true that when they knew I lived there all the time, some people looked at me as if I was out of my mind. They asked me if I was not afraid. 'Afraid of what?' I would ask. Of being cut off, having no doctor, pharmacy, shops, buses – nothing within reach, they would say. 'I have everything I need here,' was my reply, and they were speechless. Was there any point in playing the victim? I gained much respect from the elders in the village – the only ones sharing village life with me – and it puzzled me why they respected someone because of where they live rather than because of who they are. But I suppose that was tacitly implied.

I already gave him all the information that was possible to have on the house, the apartment, the village; everything. All that remained was to sign a preliminary so I gave him the name of the notary for him to contact and set the operation in motion. Apart from one minor problem we encountered along the way, everything went smoothly and we signed the preliminary after three weeks. When my neighbours came back at the end of March and learned it was sold to a Russian, they immediately said he wanted to launder his money; why else would a Russian buy a secluded little place on the mountains? It just goes to show that people always need to pass judgement and it is usually the unfavourable kind. Still, I was sure the new owners would bring added vivacity and fascination to the village.

It was time to plan the setting for my next move. My finances had been depleted so it was essential to find a bargain; the only region where that was possible was Languedoc. I looked on internet and selected what was within my budget and was vaguely acceptable. Estate agents' photos have no effect on me, mainly because they are often quite awful, one wonders if they know how to use a camera properly and with all the image viewers available, they could at least put them straight and lighten them up a tad. What interests me is the village, the general location and the exterior. The interior can always be improved but one cannot change the location or the position of the house. The only thing to do is to go and see it. No matter how diligent one is in asking all pertinent questions, there is always something that escapes one's consideration and if there are serious flaws, only a scrupulous agent will disclose them on the telephone and only if prompted. Private owners very seldom reveal the defects. I once drove miles to see a house and was not told there was a huge telephone pole just outside the front door.

The fact of moving all over again was beginning to tire and bore me and the thought of having to deal with another shabby place and another contentious community, was making me wish there was another way of managing my life. When I lived in Florence I met the son of an English Lord who asked me if I knew of an elegant place to rent. He and his family moved around the world renting magnificent places and staying as long as their desire to leave arose; sometimes a few months, other times a few years. His father is one of the largest property owners in London and when I asked him if he ever wanted to buy a property he quickly replied; 'Never! I will always rent wherever we like, anywhere in the world, then we are free to leave when we wish without any attachments.' Wonderful idea, I thought, and one I would have very happily adopted, had I been in possess of anything resembling his bank account.

When I went to visit a few properties in Languedoc, I had a déjà vu feeling, or to be more precise, a sense of being forced to repeat an action whose outcome I already knew was uncertain. After all the climbing and descending of La Rochette, the thought of living on flat land was very comforting as my knees had gone through an ordeal. There were only five properties that were suitable for my needs and budget. One of those I pretty much discarded because I could tell from the photos it needed considerable updating and it was in a village that did not sound at all attractive to me but I did not know why. For one reason or another none of the other four managed to produce any stimulus and so on the last day I went to visit the fifth; the one I had discarded. It was in a village not far from Carcassonne. It did not take me long to work out how much money it needed to be spent on so I made a low offer; it reflected my lukewarm viewpoint. If it failed then I would somehow find another solution. But they accepted and the agent assured me she would ensure the sellers signed the acceptance. I contacted the same notary who handled my first Languedoc purchase, signed a power of attorney so I would not be bound to dates and times and returned to Provence.

The interim period between signing a preliminary and the final contract is a busy time because I have to arrange the final details of the sale, begin to plan what needs to be done – and how – in the new place, arrange for the removal and deal with a lot of paperwork. There was a problem with the completion of my sale because the land registry plans were incorrect and the notary said I was responsible for appointing a *géomètre* (land surveyor) to redraw the plans and pay for the whole operation. This would have delayed completion by a month, possibly two. The reason behind this absurdity is that the plan did not correctly show the layout of my apartment in the house; above my bathroom there was a room that belonged to neighbours who probably owned the whole thing in the past and when they made the division they did not bother to correct it at the land registry. It was not impossible to complete with the status quo but the purchaser had to be told and agree to buy despite the inaccuracy. Fortunately, the Russian said he could not care less about that and so we completed. Notaries are very punctilious about such things because, when all is said and done, it is they who are held responsible. Naturally all they rely on are the documents relating to the property and the information the sellers provide, if they are honest. The notary who sold me the apartment never mentioned anything but then perhaps he was the seller's accomplice.

REPETITION OPENS DOORS

The Damned Village

Before moving I engaged a painter to repaint the interior of the house as it would have been problematic to do it afterwards. I regretted taking that decision because not only they did an awful job of it but they charged me far too much. When I arrived in the village I noticed the painter was working on the neighbour's shutters instead of painting my house. He told me he was just filling in time whilst my walls were drying which seemed an absurd excuse. I refused to pay the balance of his bill in full - much to his displeasure – because the work was sloppily done. Admittedly the walls needed at least two coats as they were multicoloured and painting the skirting was going to take some time but it did not justify the sum the painter demanded; in addition, there were no doors or windows to be done as I repainted them myself later. Luckily my dear friend Brian was on a visit from Wales and when the painter looked up at him towering over his small build, he changed his tune and suddenly became compliant. Had I been 6 feet 2 inches tall perhaps he would have acquiesced to me too but then I would have had to be a male as well. I also had an unfortunate encounter with a carpenter who was supposed to strip the wooden floor in the bedrooms. He made such a mess that I was obliged to pay for the work twice; the carpenter who threatened me if I did not pay him in cash, and for a new floor covering to hide the botching he had done. I was so frustrated and disappointed for having to deal with another set of short-sighted, dishonest rogues, that I broke down in tears. When things turn out badly at the beginning, it is unlikely they go very well later.

I met my neighbour the first day I arrived with the removal people. From the first glance, it was clear she was going to give me a hard time. The house is in a narrow cul-de-sac but I could just manage to drive in front of my door and turn the car round without reversing all the way back. In front of the house there are the ruins of a 13th century castle and the medieval church so when I looked out the western side the view was full of history and charm. On the eastern side the mountains of Alaric in the distance afforded a different but equally captivating view. The mountain is 600 meters high (more a hill in my view than a mountain) and bears the name of a

Visigoth King, Alaric II, who is believed to be buried there and according to legend, a Roman treasure is hidden somewhere beneath the mountain but nobody has ever found it. Even if someone had found it, would they shout it from the top of the mountain? The village was built in a defensive circular style in the Middle Ages when the area around Carcassonne was almost always in the midst of bloody crusades and vicious feuds. Does it happen to you that the first moment you arrive in a new place, you are immediately introduced to its secret essence? It feels like an impression, a sort of subtle intuition that either transmits a desire to stay or to leave. I was beginning to understand why I had discarded the house even before visiting it.

The property had some advantages; the view was quite good and there were no neighbours in front. But little by little the drawbacks began to manifest themselves without respite. The first was my next-door neighbour; her first words to me were 'you can't park your car here.' The following day she told me where to put my potted plants outside my front door. I ignored what she said and bought her some flowers in the hope she might change her tune. I carried on my refurbishing in the house and continued to park the car outside my door. She told me once more to park elsewhere and so I made a cake and offered her half. When after a few weeks she renewed her bullying then I changed my tune. I asked her if she had been engaged by the Mairie to supervise parking arrangements in the village to which she replied '*non.*'

'Do you own all the houses in the street?' I asked.

'*Non,*' she replied.

'Then on what authority do you order me to not park here when all the other people in the street put their car outside their houses?'

'Because I park mine in the square and so should you. I do not like cars near my house.'

'And I do not like to be ordered about and bullied so unless you want to go to war with me, I suggest you keep your antagonism to yourself and avoid talking to me from now on.' The whole thing made me feel tired and I remembered a journalist once said that the French are quarrelsome and prefer to separate into antagonistic irreconcilable groups fighting each other rather than stand together against common enemies. She could have welcomed me as a newcomer and profited from a new relation instead of turning me into an enemy. But there it was.

A friend of mine whom I met in Provence some years back – Odile - decided to come and live near me and asked me if I could find her a house to rent in the village which I did find through acquaintances though I told her about my initial experience and hoped it would not happen to her. She was only going to use the place as a pied-à-terre so the quality of the neighbourhood concerned her very little. We went shopping together and had walks along the Canal du Midi with Mel, lunches in charming little restaurants and exchanged stimulating conversations. Odile is French and has travelled extensively and though that does not necessarily change a person or make them better, she has an open mind and can laugh about her fellow citizens. However, Odile was not in fact there very often and when she was absent, it made me realise how important it is to cherish the time we have with good friends.

The house was fairly comfortable and after a friend came to visit from England, summer was well into the scorching 35° which made sleeping only possible at around 5am when the night finally cooled off. The roof was not insulated and the house was south-west facing so despite the wind, that seemed to be missing on the hottest days, the place was a sizzling oven during July and August. One of the southern characteristics is to spend summer days with the shutters closed and escape to lakes, streams, beaches; any place where there is water in the hope of finding some solace. The result is that most villages have an air of utter abandonment during the day but come the night, they all come alive with fervency and commotion so that when one is exhausted and wants to sleep, the neighbours are setting up the tables for the feast. My bedroom window was at the back of the house, overlooking a large property with a pool that was rented out by the week. The guests paid to have a good time so between the noise of constant splashing in the water, the incessant ear-splitting music and the strident laughter which went on well into the early morning hours, my endurance was put through a strenuous test. It was nothing, however, compared to what was to come. On the 14th of July – Bastille Day – the fireworks were displayed on the plateau of the castle ruins in front of my house. Had someone told me that the house would tremble every time an aerial shell was sent off with a bang, I would have vacated the street and sought temporary shelter. Between the noise, the smoke and the flashing lights, even if I had bolted all the windows and doors, it was like being in the middle of a ferocious combat zone. Mel was terrorised; his tongue was sticking out and his body was shaking violently, he was trying to find refuge under the bed but with no avail. I gave him some herbal sedative but even that had no effect. It was probably the worst night in both our memories, though I suspect dogs have more of an imprint than a memory.

Surviving through that summer of 2015 was not an easy thing. I said earlier that August is not my favourite month and one of the reasons for disliking it is that having lived in hot climates, it is in August that torrid days alternate with potent thunderstorms, turning the atmosphere into an oppressive tropical hothouse. Landscapes are parched, people are stressed and if you want to eat out, you pay first class rates for second-rate meals. So I always stay at home but that year I formed a bond with myself; I vowed never to spend another August in a place like that. There are two months that make me give a sigh of relief when they are over; one is August and the other is December. During those two months, one for holidays and the other for celebrations, we humans behave like senseless puppets who keep replicating the same scenarios over and over, and the irony is that they are the highlights of the year.

One positive aspect of the village was that there was a small park and that is where I used to take Mel for walks. In an attempt to break the monotonous habit, sometimes I went along the railway where the vineyards and the views provided a pleasant change but wherever I went, there often was a dog – or dogs – who systematically attacked Mel with aggressive force. Once we were quietly promenading down a street, a door opened and a man with a cigarette in his mouth came out followed by a raging dog who went straight for Mel's neck. The walking stick I made at La Rochette came in very handy in this kind of situation; not to use as a weapon but as a deterrent and it served as comfort for me.

In France love of animals is a very complicated matter. There was a time when cows and horses lived next door to their owners, they even made holes in the walls between the stable and the house to allow the animals to see what was going on. They were treated as members of the family; they were sung to, dressed up for special occasions and given names; their manure was nearly more prized than meat. But alongside this, they also behaved in a brutal and vicious manner toward animals; hens were used as target practice, dogs were starved so that they would make violent guards; horses were worked hard until they collapsed and bourgeois travellers on Mediterranean ships entertained themselves by shooting dolphins. Today there are more than eight million dogs in France and the treatment they receive from their owners covers the whole spectrum of human compassion at one end and brutish cruelty at the other. I have met people who pamper and care for their pets in an obsessive way and others who simply use them for their personal needs without giving a thought to their welfare. There was a time when anything that crawled, walked or flew, was destined to end up in someone's casserole. More creativity had been deployed in the eradication of certain species than the guillotine, for example. Birds were particularly relished. In Provence a songbird stew was an absolute delicacy and the fact that birds ate harmful insects was of little consideration to the locals, even if they knew they did. The cunning ways I which they caught birds well exceeded the ways in which they preserved them, so much so that in the 18th century a voyager may well have treated it like an ecological disaster. Women were particularly skilful in eliminating them; they could kill hundreds of birds in a few minutes by biting their necks.

When one receives antagonism and resentment from others, it is very difficult to open up to them and show them amity, unless one is a Saint. The hostility and rudeness in that village surpassed anything I have ever encountered. Once I was quietly walking along the pavement with Mel and put my foot on the road in an attempt to cross it but withdrew my foot when I saw a car speeding up toward me. The driver stopped, put his head outside the window, shouted various insults at me and then drove off. I have lived in India and some rough places in the Middle East but this sort of thing never happened to me. Even people in the street were shocked and one apologised to me as if he felt somehow responsible, if only for sharing the same race with that brute. As a result of all the upsetting experiences in the village, I was even afraid to walk Mel after dark and just kept to the familiar streets around my house.

In front of my house, as I already said, was the medieval church and the remains of the ancient castle. The two ways out of my street were either around the church or toward the entrance of the cul-de-sac. Whichever way, that was the highest point in the village and the wind gusts could on occasion very well sweep me away. In the evening when I took Mel for his last walk, I tended to avoid going around the church as there were two very dark unlit corners and twice found men urinating against the wall. Not that this activity was in any way threatening but both times Mel got a spray of urine on him – as well as on my shoes - because one is forced to walk quite close to the walls when bypassing the church. It was clear this urination business had been going on during the previous centuries as the walls bore large dark brown traces but it was surprising to find the activity was still being performed today though I should have guessed it was judging by the odour the walls emanated. France has been described as 'the land of the pissoir' and despite the installation of countless public mobile toilets, some Frenchmen still prefer taking their piss *en plein air*. In that village it seemed to be particularly relished.

At the end of August, I was convinced I had to get away from the South and settle in the cool North where people are well-educated and discreet. *Yes, here we go again!* The house was the best it could ever be, save blowing it up and rebuilding it. As always, what to a person is a major flaw, to someone else it can be an asset, and this adage was going to be proved right. As well as reading five books during August, I also finished off some things in the house that had been suspended for lack of enthusiasm on my part. I would have painted but finding inspiration was like getting on a train in the middle of the ocean. As it always happens before selling a property, doubts set in at night; I lied in bed going through all the things that to me were negative and almost convinced myself that it would never sell. Then in the morning I got up with renewed confidence and kept going most of the day on a steady note of optimism.

At the beginning of September I asked a local agent to value the house and as usual it was exactly as I estimated it. I advertised it on the English language site as well as locally but had no feedback at all for several weeks. Then an email arrived from a woman in America who wanted more information and photos. Further down the street there was an American couple who had been living in the village for some years so I thought, why not another American. We exchanged a number of emails and the lady came all the way from New Orleans to visit my house. At least that is what she declared. I believed her because she immediately struck me as not only extremely charming but also well-grounded. She stayed the best part of a day with me and, after promising me to get back with a written offer, she flew to London to meet her sister before returning to US. In this type of situation, it is not easy to assess a person's character, to tell whether they are genuine and mean what they say. In general I always do believe what people say but doubts sometimes set in, because of the unfortunate experiences one has had and because the business of selling one's house can be emotionally unsettling. However, when someone flies across the world and spends most part of a day in my house because they want to get the feel of the place, it is safe enough to deduce they are serious. And indeed she was. That charming woman, Fiona, sent me an email with the written offer, exactly as promised.

There have only been two houses where I did not feel a compelling need to move as soon as possible; this was not one of them. So, despite the offer was low considering all the furniture she wished to buy, I accepted and was thrilled at the thought of leaving that unfriendly atmosphere once and for all. So great was my desire to abandon the South that my search instinctively steered me to the highest point in the North - or nearly. I had been in Brittany once for a holiday and apart from the rain, it seemed a pleasant enough place to me. But then it was a short vacation and it concerned the Morbihan coast only. What was the rest of Brittany like? I was certainly going to find out.

One of the things I try to notice and consider are the 'signs,' or hidden messages that one gets along life's path. The first time I drove up to Brittany to find a house, I was accompanied by my friend Odile who kindly offered to help with the trip and the search. We spent a week in a gîte spending our days running from one place to another, getting constantly lost on the Breton rural roads and at the end returning to Languedoc without any result. The first thing that happened when we arrived and I opened the door, was a raging dog that suddenly appeared from nowhere and attacked Mel. The poor darling was already exhausted from having spent 860 km in the car and did not know how to deal with the abrupt aggression. Fortunately, the owner came along and got her dog off Mel's neck before he had a chance to snap it. Odile, who had heard about the terrific dog encounters, had now witnessed one and was thoroughly appalled. I suddenly felt terribly miserable; I was about to sell my house – this was in itself a positive thing altogether – but had no idea if and when I would find a new place in that distant and strange region. Was the fact that my trip proved fruitless and disappointing mean that there was a meaningful reason behind it?

It is said that bad choices have huge negative consequences, but is it really true - that is to say, is it our ethical, religious or rational self that decides it was a bad choice or is it because time has proved it to be so? My life has been an endless sequence of choices; some made hastily, some pondered, others motivated by necessity but all of them have, in one way or another, taught me something, even if it was not immediately apparent. Scientists would say this is not true; they would say that what causes our wanting to make a certain choice instead of another is exclusively due to the biochemical processes in our brain, we merely act out that choice hence giving us the illusion that it was we who caused it. But that is another story. There are only two decisions I have taken which I regret still today but then it is because of them that other events have succeeded themselves and initiated new possibilities. It is only with experience and hindsight that some aspects of these choices become clear. One bad choice could have generated sad repercussions but it could also have been the ground in which new seeds were planted, the produce of which would only later be manifested. What I am trying to say is that clear-cut and unquestionable statements are often the result of shallow considerations.

A COUNTRY WITHIN A NATION

A Lighter Shade of Bleak

There was no choice but to make another trip to Brittany – that is if I wanted to go and live there. It was also necessary to change the area in which to search for a property. On the first visit I had concentrated on southern Morbihan, being the warmest and sunniest area of Bretagne but it is also the most expensive and though there were a couple that could have ultimately done the trick, there was nothing that 'spoke' to me. The trip did however leave a good impression of the area. Coming from the arid South, it was very refreshing to see great oak trees and luscious forests as well as green fields. Like when we look at the fast-moving landscape on a train journey, our perception of a place can only be proportioned to the superficiality of our observation. We see what we want to see in that particular moment. And so it was when I saw Brittany on my first visit. Just like someone who has been forced to live in total darkness, even a crack in the wall that suddenly lets in a beam of light will seem like a resplendent sun, so was my need to be surrounded by a soothing and natural environment presenting me the lens through which I saw Bretagne.

Between my first and second visits, a couple of houses appeared on the market; one of these had the sort of charming decadence that appeals to me. It means it had what it takes for turning it into an appealing transformation. Some houses are old but have either been stripped of all original features or they were poorly built in the first place. The other house for sale was very functional because it was plain pied but it was as common as five fingers on a hand. The area these houses were located was more inland and it was one of the many parts of Brittany I did not know. The closest town was Josselin, a medieval small city with timbered houses and the Canal de Nantes à Brest flowing through it.

The agent who showed me the house tried to put pressure on me by saying that at that price it was going to sell very quickly so there was no time to lose. I ignored him and tried to forget I too had no time to lose for I needed to find a house but had to keep my cool and make the right choice. The owner was in the house and he was very affable though his replies to my questions laid in a grey area where truth and lie are easily indefinable. He said they lived in Paris and used the house as a second home so had little time to do any improvements. He also whispered to me that there was an offer that he was presently considering but had not made up his mind. That type of comment is very annoying as it is usually intended to achieve two results via the devious route. I was told I could have all the furniture at no extra price and there were even some logs left in the cellar to light up the fireplace and warm the house when I arrived. There was clearly no heating - save for the fireplace - but there was also no bathroom, except for a hand-basin and a lavatory. I worked out in my mind how much it would cost me to do the necessary works and made an offer according to what my budget allowed, taking into account the taxes and notary's fees that had to be included. I could tell the owner was trying to sell it to me and it was clear he saw me in his mind as a credulous, single English woman who lapped up everything that was thrown at her.

The offer was immediately accepted and after signing the preliminary I returned to Languedoc. There was not much time to find some artisans, a place to stay while the renovation was being done and some removers. It never occurred to me that in Brittany things are different from any other region, even if my travels have demonstrated that each region is indeed inimitably diverse. How different Brittany is, was going to be revealed to me. The village Mairie gave me the name of an artisan whom I called but just talking to him on the telephone convinced me that, apart from being rather pricy, he and I were not going to get along well. Fortunately, I found an Englishman – Dave - on internet who promised to be a great help and though he himself was not a DIY expert, he could propose people for specific jobs. Once again, I was taking a leap in the dark and whilst in the past I have always believed that when one does that only goods things can happen, now it was time to revise that concept. Putting a step in the dark is one thing; fleeing somewhere to avoid where one is, is quite another. It is like men and women who seek a partner because they are desperate and unable to be alone. What they will attract is another who is also desperate and unable to be alone and whilst they may not know it – in fact they undoubtedly do not – that is the recipe for a catastrophic relationship.

Brittany was never intended to be the solution to my problem in the South; it was a far enough away destination that promised to restore trust in human-*kind*. It is easy to forget for a moment that human beings do not change just because they live 900 miles away or on a different latitude; they are merely a variation on the same theme. And in any case, what did I expect? Moving to Brittany was going to be expensive but was lucky to have found Paul who goes up and down France all the time and he agreed to do it for a very reasonable price. Having a small van, he needed to do two trips but it worked out in the end and the price did not change. When it arrived, I had my furniture deposited in the centre of the living room whilst trying to keep what I might need at arm's length. Easier said than done!

Once more I had moved in the winter – January 2016 – and commencing works with the cold and rain was not the happiest scenario but it was not going to put me off. Armed with willpower and tenacity, I got up in the morning when it was still dark, took Mel for his walk, did my daily exercises, had breakfast and drove to the house, put my gloves on and started working. Dave had introduced an excellent plumber who could begin installing the kitchen and bathroom as soon as possible. There was no water in the kitchen, as the sink was in the entrance hall, and there was no hot water tank. The house needed painting and the electricity needed updating. What I did not know however, was that there had been a leakage in the hand basin pipe that, before soaking the toilet and kitchen floor, had infiltrated through the cellar underneath and damaged the supporting beams. This must have happened quite a while back and it is hard to believe the owner was not aware of it, even if the floor was covered with lino. In the purchase contract there is always the clause '*l'action en garantie des vices cachés*' – action for the guarantee of hidden defects – which protects the purchaser but the vendors can always say they were not aware of the defect and it is difficult to prove they were, so I did not even give it a thought. In any case, by this time I was well vaccinated against these failings and had no intention of embarking on the legal route.

The first thing to do was to reinforce the beams in the cellar which supported half of the house's floor, then substitute the old floor in the kitchen and toilet for a new one. These works were not provided for in my expenditure calculation. I was obliged to engage the only carpenter available in order to get the work done immediately and when one is pressed for time it is almost always inevitable one finds a profiteer who exploits the situation. The carpenter demanded to be paid in cash and did a lousy job but I got him to come back and put it right. Dave and I started painting the downstairs in the most appalling clutter; half the house floor missing, the other half covered with my furniture, workers who had to tread along wires, cables and pipes, but we managed somehow. The continuous rain was not helping as the house was unheated and getting damper by the minute. If there was not Mel to be taken out for a walk I would have avoided driving to the gîte backward and forward four times a day but leaving him in the car or the house was not an option.

The plumber Dave introduced to me was proving to be a real treasure; he was fast, worked well and was extremely pleasant as a person. In just a week he installed a new bathroom upstairs where the third bedroom would have been; it was a small room and exactly in the middle between the other two so it was the perfect place to convert it into a bathroom. He also fixed the kitchen sink and put in a new water heater in the cellar. In just over seven days he made the house habitable, at least in terms of essential plumbing and on top of everything he was very reasonably priced. The electrician, who was presented to me by the plumber, was equally efficient but rather surly; we communicated in codes and even that was hard work, but he got better as time went on. Perhaps that is how Bretons are, I said to myself, they need time to warm up to someone.

By the middle of February – a month after the renovation began – I had put the furniture in place and the house looked as it had been lived in for a long time. The garden was just the right size; the grass was going to need mowing but Dave could take care of that. There was an apple tree in the centre and I had hung fat and seeds balls for the birds on two branches; it was an immense pleasure to sit in the kitchen, look out of the window and watch the flock of blue tits, starlings and sparrows eat ravenously, fly all over the place and chirp like there was no tomorrow. That became for me the highlight of the day and turned breakfast and lunch into very special and enjoyable moments. I rarely had supper and in any case it would have been too dark by then to see outside. Alongside the pleasure of feeding birds and watching them being thankful, there was also the regret of knowing that one day I would leave and they would have to find another restaurant.

From my garden I could see the village church that is just across the road. It is a large ancient building with lovely stained glass windows and spire. During the week there were choir practices and then a lot of singing was performed on Sundays. Brittany was one of the most stalwartly Catholic regions in all of France and they probably placed more importance on Saints than on God Himself. Every village – even the smallest – has a huge church and various crosses planted here and there. I was curious to see the interior of the church and chose a Sunday Mess to do it. As I entered half way through the Mess and had no intention in staying until the end, I picked the last solitary pew. Almost all the men were on one side of the nave and women on the other, which was curious, and they all seemed to be over fifty years old. I was about to leave near the end of the Mess when the Priest descended from the altar and walked down the central nave; he stopped beside me and asked me why I was sitting there. That is an odd question, I thought, and was slightly annoyed by it as in my opinion I had done nothing to deserve his attention. Everyone turned their heads toward me and whilst my instinct was to apologise and leave, my rational self, claimed an explanation. 'Would you please care to enlighten me on the reason for your question?' I asked in my best French. The priest explained that everyone should sit together not in isolation because it gives a sense of dispersion and it struck me as an obvious Catholic-style answer. Mother church wants all her children to stick together like a mob of sheep and as I was straying from the flock, I was setting a bad example. Part of me wanted to get into a debate about democracy, religion and freedom of choice but I simply thanked him and made my way to the door. None of the church-goers made any attempt to smile, they stared at me as if I was a foreign sinner seeking pardon in vain for my criminal malefactions. That was my second close encounter with the Breton mentality and character. The first one was a stern-looking couple in a car who stopped alongside me and Mel and asked me where the car salesman was; I only started explaining that I had moved recently when they just drove off without a thank you or a goodbye, let alone a smile.

It may be partly because the people in the church were seniors but I had the impression that there was not much entente between Breton men and women; the latter were regarded as equal but only in so far as hard work was concerned. There was a time when men went off to sea or to pastures and women had to be responsible for the house, the crops, the family and everything else. They were more comrades than sweethearts. Sentimentality may have played a role in past generations but the main reason for marrying was to consolidate inherited land rights. Sometimes this meant marrying a cousin or a half-sister. There are hundreds of chauvinistic proverbs that confirm women were treated no better than beasts of burden. One from Brittany says; 'a dead wife, a living horse, a wealthy man.'

Young people today have much more at their disposal for breaking away from old traditions but in my observation of Brittany, either the majority of Bretons are seniors or they have changed very little indeed. Without wishing to generalise or exaggerate, the only persons who have had a smile on their faces have been outsiders. Most of the Bretons have had a tough life and probably still have but that is not the chief reason for their cheerless countenance; it is something that is imbued in their psyche. The roots of the gloom are the long years of precariousness and hardship, bad luck, migration and ignorance. When I arrived in Brittany I smiled at people but they never reciprocated so I gradually gave it up. One time when I smiled at a man in a supermarket, he looked at me severely and told me he was married. That puffed-up narcissist cured me of my smile.

The dismal weather does not help, nor does the fact that so many British have occupied their region, renovated their properties by importing workmen from UK instead of using local artisans and caused real estate prices to increase beyond many Bretons' buying power. Today the market is crammed with properties for sale, a lot of them are in need of total renovation and look quite dismal; at the higher end of the scale they have been sumptuously renovated by English owners who now, for political or financial reasons, need to sell. However, I believe there will always be keen purchasers of properties in Brittany because it is a charming region, particularly along the coastline. Parisians who have a sailing boat and a sea-view cottage, will be unlikely to let them go because that is where they can get away from it all and be in touch with a wild and stunning environment.

One of my neighbours was a Welsh woman living there most of the year. She was very helpful to me when I applied for a telephone line and broadband but they were not forthcoming and she let me use her wi-fi. As I got to know her it became clear to me why she felt completely at home in Brittany. She told me she spoke welsh but despite the fact she had been living in France for many years, she did not speak French, save the usual pleasantries. I never thought of asking her if she spoke Breton, a language closely related to welsh, both being Celtic. Breton - an insular Celtic language - was the one used by the upper classes until the 12th century and then became the language of commoners. For the natives of Brittany, having to learn French must have been a mortifying and humiliating experience; they loved their language so much they still hang on to it today with a firm grip. If you are familiar with Brittany you know that road signs are in both languages; Breton and French. Today it is the only living Celtic language that is not recognized by the government as an official or regional language. The French State refuses to give it any importance and even if it was the Celtic Language spoken by the highest number of persons, it is now endangered.

Dave proved to be an invaluable help to me as he had lived in the village for some years and could supply me with unsolicited information about the people, their habits and peculiarities. I was told there was a tart in the village who had the habit of leaving the curtains open when she was available. French villages do really cater for a variety of needs, albeit some may not be advertised on the council's page. I asked Dave if it was normal in Brittany to demand a fee when supplying an estimate for a job, the reason being that two workers asked me fifty euros for quotation I had required. I did not pay them because it did not make sense but to be doubly sure I went to ask the Maire if it was indeed a local custom. He replied that it was not and that was the first time he heard of such bizarre practice. It was not, however, the first or second time they would insist I pay it. One of the reasons I gave myself was that they needed work and to avoid wasting time giving estimates without a return, they decided to adopt that method in an effort to at least cover the transport costs, but then again that may have been the very reason why they did not get many jobs confirmations which they would have done if they offered to refund the fifty euros once they were appointed for the work. But no sign of that.

I finally got the telephone and internet after I despaired for a long while. Orange, who cover most of the national network, sent me an estimate of 1.300 euros for supplying me with a telephone line. That got my undivided attention. The thing was that my next-door neighbour had a line and it was just a matter of extending the cable into my house. Or so I thought. They told me they had to 'create' a new line which involved, inter alia, demolishing the pavement along the road. So, back I went to the Maire and enquired whether I could have some elucidation as to this scandalous request. I was told that as the Orange telephone lines were antiquated, they took advantage of new clients to shell out large sums of money to pay for the new lines. I then called another operator (Free) and they said it was bollocks; they would supply me with a line and broadband within a few days for 35 euros. And they did. Needless to say, I became an immediate fan of Free and everything was hanky-dory. I wrote registered letters to all the Orange addresses I could get hold of expressing my surprise and disappointment at their shocking request but they insisted in charging me 114 euros for the time they spent in preparing the quotation. A cheque arrived in the post for the same amount from a Paris branch. My understanding is that the Orange office in Brittany were inflexible about receiving that amount so an intelligent manager somewhere decided to refund me in advance thereby equating the amount. It is incredibly frustrating to dispose of anonymous addresses all over France without ever the name of a person to whom one can write or telephone, and to make it worse the Orange addresses regularly change so one has the impression of being contingent on a phantom roaming entity with unrestricted monopoly on one's personal data.

Once I had the front and back doors changed for new PVC ones, there was no more wind and rain coming into the house and everything was now completed. The question of what I was going to do began to hover in the air. It was spring 2016. The hydrangeas in the garden were in full blossom and grown so high they were almost trees; the roses in the neighbour's side were leaning over my garden fence on the left and the neighbour's azaleas were swathing over the wall on the right. It was a florescence feast the moment I put the foot out of the door. Soil in being mainly acidic in Brittany, plants such as rhododendrons, azaleas and camellias thrive and the temperate and humid climate helps them grow to amazing heights. I was delighted to discover that Bretons love flowers and it is rare to find houses without potted plants on their windowsill and blooming gardens. But even all that flowering delight would not inspire me to paint. I went to the coast a few times hoping that the sea air and wild beauty might rush me to my brushes and canvases but no; nothing. It had been a while since the desire to paint brushed against me. I tried finishing my pending novel but my eyes would stare at the screen of my pc as if I was comatose and my hands would touch the keyboard in vain. The time had come to start packing.

I telephoned a Leggett agency and a very pleasant man came to give me an estimate. To my surprise it was higher than expected, though I had no idea what a house like mine could sell for in Brittany. He also said that he had recently started working with Leggett and had therefore limited experience but had seen many houses and mine would sell very quickly. Just to be sure the price was correct, I also telephoned a French estate agent and his valuation was much lower. Perhaps the right value of the house was somewhere between the two but as I was not pressed, I decided to put it for sale at a slightly inferior price than Leggett's valuation; it could always be adjusted later. And so I gave it to Leggett on a non-exclusive mandate and I advertised it myself on green-acres. Quite soon after there was a couple from Cornwall who enquired from my ad and were so enthralled about the place they decided to take an overnight boat to Roscoff and go back the next day. They were coming exclusively to visit my house, they said. When this kind of thing happens, it always makes me feel enthusiastic but also slightly nervous because someone had undertaken a long journey and will be disappointed. That is one of the reasons I avoid misleading people and tell them as much truth as possible about my house. If anything is left out it is merely an ancillary detail such as my neighbour hangs her knickers to dry in front of my window or the gutter creaks when it is very windy.

The couple from Cornwall visited the house and took time to ask questions and look around on their own. At the end of the visit they offered me the asking price and said they were thrilled they did not make the trip for nothing; my property corresponded exactly to the description I gave and to their expectations. It was not the first time this happened to me but it still caught me unawares as I did not expect things to move as such a vertiginous speed. They left and once again I was thrown in a befuddled state of mind. Were they serious about their offer; would I hear from them again? The next day they sent me an email, as promised but the content was disheartening. They wrote that they loved the house but they spoke to their accountant who was extremely cautious about the purchase. The referendum was going to take place three weeks later - 23 June 2016 – and he suggested they wait for the outcome because if Britain was leaving Europe things would be uncertain. They promised they would get in touch after the referendum if nothing changed, and we all know what the result was. I perfectly understood their reluctance but wondered why they did not think of it before, they would have avoided a useless trip.

A week later I was contacted by another couple from Wales who also expressed their firm interest and decision to travel immediately and view the property. It did cross my mind whether I should ask them if they did not prefer to wait after the referendum but I generally give people the benefit of the doubt that they plan their journeys with intelligence. When they arrived they immediately showed their interest in an unambiguous manner. After much talking and visiting, they said they would go to the local bar and discuss it between themselves and return with their decision. When they came back they offered slightly less than the asking price including a lot of the furniture and I accepted. They insisted I call the notary and arrange the signing of the preliminary whilst they were staying for a few days so that they could leave knowing everything was taken care of. I called the notary's office – the same one who sold me the house – and told them the preliminary had to be signed within the next three days to which they replied; 'oh no, we cannot do that, we are very busy, perhaps next week.' To which I replied, 'never mind, I will find another notary. Goodbye.' The woman caught me before I hang up and said; 'perhaps I can arrange it…give me a minute please.' And so it goes.

The lovely couple from Wales – Yvonne and Kevin – had brought with them all the documents that a voracious notary might require, which made the signing of the preliminary victorious. I asked them if they were not worried about Brexit and they replied that even if Britain left Europe it would take years before things were resolved and in any case it would not affect their wish to buy a house in France. How can one not like people like that? One of the things I agreed to leave in the house was a gilt mirror I had bought in Hong Kong many years back and as well as being very unusual and gorgeous, it had managed to stay in one piece despite numerous moves around the world. It was what made the living room so charming. I could not take it away even if they did not ask for it in their list of furniture and fittings.

Now that the sale was set in motion, I could go to visit my brother in Italy who was very poorly so I booked a flight from Nantes and landed in Milan with Easyjet before the start of summer. I found a friendly kennel for Mel not far from Guer which is on the route to the airport. The days when I was more on a plane than on land had long gone and had not realised how many people are on the move now that flights are cheaper and frequent. I was astonished by the crowds in the airports and the number of cars in the parking lots. Perhaps people should start taking the problem of overpopulation more seriously. Seeing my dear brother was a wonderful treat though it was painful to find him so changed and suffering; it was alas going to be the last time we would meet but I did not know that at the time.

Yvonne and Kevin proved to be not only charming but so kind and pleasant to be with. I was delighted that they liked the house and we have met since for lunch a couple of times. I hope we will be able to meet up again in the future even if it means going back to Brittany but perhaps they will decide to venture into the South. Dave has been appointed as a caretaker when they are not in residence and it seems a perfect arrangement.

A VARIATION ON ANOTHER THEME

Farming is a Hopeful Occupation

When I returned from Italy I started looking for the next place. My experience in Brittany had been somewhat brief and confused, I had the feeling that perhaps it was not yet time to leave. In addition, the recent renovation work plus the various problems of settling in, had tired and stressed me so it was not the moment to undertake another major relocation. What was needed was a small place with a garden and no stairs. There was not much time to dawdle as the purchasers wanted to move in for their holidays in July and it was already May. I searched internet and found a small place further inland toward Pontivy. When I saw it with the agent it was quite discouraging but it was the only one that corresponded to some of my criteria so I made an offer and it was accepted. There was something about it that dampened my enthusiasm, though the latter was now becoming very scarce anyway. There was something about the road, the farming land around it and the fact that was semi-detached, even if the neighbour could be easily avoided, that sent me messages of apprehension but it was too late to change my mind and I was going to make the best of it. I have learned to always trust my intuition and generally act accordingly but sometimes necessity has conditioned my choices; this was one of them.

The garden was bigger than I needed but in
Brittany land is more available than in the South
and certainly at lesser cost; in fact what agents
define as *'petit jardin'* is what in the South
would be called a portion of land. The roof
needed complete renovation and the septic tank
had to be changed. These were major works but
had been included in my budget when I made the
offer. There was also a hangar in the garden that
was larger than the house; it had been used for
farm machinery and it could become a garage
and workshop. This time I was going to move not
in the autumn but in the summer. As most of my
furniture had been sold with the house, there was
just the right amount to fill this much smaller

pavilion and I would have to buy a small sofa-bed as there was only one bedroom. If the idea of having guests crossed my mind, it was going to be proved unfounded. Dave had a van and he helped me move to the new place and also gave me a hand to repaint the walls and get rid of some rubbish.

I had already investigated the possible companies for the roof and the septic tank and as soon as I moved in, I contacted them for a quote. The first person I met was the director of a large and varied enterprise that carried out and dealt with all sorts of operations, including animal farming, sanitation and road works. And his company was just half a mile away from me. His name was Gilles and he was such a pleasant and helpful man that he literally lifted my spirits. The garden was in almost total darkness due to general neglect and because three hazel trees had grown too large for the space, thus obscuring the whole plot. As much as it displeased me to have to do it, they needed to be cut down and so I asked for a quote from some garden specialists. They told me it would cost at least 2.000 euros and proceeded to describe how complicated it was; they needed to bring a small lorry, get rid of the branches, clean up the mess... etcetera and how that kind of work demanded special attention, so it could well cost a lot more in the end. After they left I went to look at myself in the mirror just to verify there was not 'idiot' written on my forehead. Had I been a man instead of a foreign woman, it is sure they would not have given that quote. Gilles came and did everything in one afternoon and charged me 300 euros. I wondered how many credulous English clients had fallen in that trap and no wonder they imported their own workers from UK. It was obviously also a question of communication as all the Brits I met in Brittany did not speak French but a lot of Bretons had to learn English, whether they liked it or not, if they wanted to sell or provide services to the Brits.

There were times when I would have given anything to have a garden; I imagined myself planting roses, all the aromatic herbs and yellow tulips in the spring. Now that I had one, I could not bring myself to do anything with it. Even if it was going to be excavated for the installation of the septic tank, there was still half the garden available to satisfy any keen horticulturist. All I could do was to look at it and wish it was covered with pebbles. Before the end of August, Gilles had already finished the septic system and despite him insisting the garden should have been seeded for the lawn because it would have been nicer, he accepted to deliver huge quantities of gravel instead and thus made my day. There was no mowing to do and every time it rained – which was every other day – there was no mess in the house to clean up. I replanted two of the hydrangeas that had been uprooted and left on the ground for at least a week I was not sure they would survive but amazingly enough they did.

The land on the other side of the garden was agricultural and the farmer had already harvested it; now he was preparing the soil for the next lot of crops. One day I was putting the washing on the line in the garden and noticed the tractor was depositing chemical fertilizers in his field. The smell was so strong, it took three successive washes to eliminate it from my laundry. Had I known it, I would not have left it on the line and certainly not chosen that day to do my washing. I could not go out of the house because of the smell and I had the distinct impression it was affecting my respiratory system. I immediately researched farming in Brittany and discovered that air pollution created on industrial farms from the application of nitrogen-based fertilizer contributes heavily to both illness and a reduction in soil carbon. The chemical products that were used in the field spilled over and permeated my garden and that is why I never noticed any worm or, in fact, any living organism in the soil. It was like as if the earth was dead. The depletion of rich carbon sources from the soil means that it cannot grow anything unless it is fertilized with chemical products, like synthetic nitrogen. If it was left to regenerate itself for many years perhaps it would have a chance but people demand increased crop yields all the time and this requires chemical fertilizers.

The industries which produce them are always saying that they have people's best interests at heart but in reality what they have at heart is enriching their bank accounts. If there was ever the mildest interest in me for gardening, what I was witnessing around me certainly gave it the final blow.

Living in the centre of Brittany was revealing to be quite a discovery. The country is abounding with animal farms; pigs, poultry and cattle. There are huge hangars everywhere; they are equipped with automatic feeders and devoid of any opening to the outside world. They are a constant reminder of the miserable life animals are subjected to in their loathsome interiors. The fact that these places also exuded strong odours was something that did not even bother me, so strong was my grief for the sorry fate of the poor animals. I am not a regular meat-eater but had I been, this experience, coupled with all the shocking photos and videos on social networks, would have been enough to make me change my diet. It may sound pathetic but I was so affected by the whole industrial breeding business that I ventured outside only for essential necessities. Taking Mel for walks was a problem and I preferred to drive to a small park with a pond every day rather than promenade around the neighbouring fields and hear the loud mooing of the cattle, the weeping snort of the pigs or the shooting blasts of the hunters. In the gardens there were never any dogs walking which was so disappointing for Mel who never got to meet any friends. In fact the park was generally deserted but in a region that was so verdant anyway, a leafy spot was hardly a sought-after novelty.

The house was gradually revealing a rising damp problem. It was partly due to the fact that it had been shut for long periods but principally because the façades had been covered by cement rendering which impeded the walls from breathing and because the foundations had no insulation at all. There were treatments but they did not promise long-lasting results and besides, I was not going to be there long enough to have them done. Luckily it was now September and the house continued to get plenty of aeration but it rained frequently which added to the dampness and with the autumn and winter approaching, it was not going to improve at all. I plastered all the cracks along the borders of the foundation to avoid the rain seeping in beneath the house and aggravating the humidity but am not sure how much that helped. The bathroom was on the north side of the house and whatever I did, the dark damp patches on the wall would always reappear. The roof had been recovered with new slate tiles and the woodwork had been replaced; at least that was now waterproof. The artisan who carried out the work was a real professional and a very kind man. He was born in Bretagne and lived all his 75 years in Bretagne; he had a constant smile on his face and a keen sense of humour, so much so that when he finished the work I really missed him. In fact, he and Gilles were both so helpful, expert, considerate and jovial that they made all the other useless rogues who tried to swindle me fade in obscurity.

I was starting to feel traces of melancholy and before it could set in and affect me, it was necessary to review my situation and find solutions. I had no friends in the area; I was isolated in the middle of a bucolic and dreary landscape with huge tractors going backward and forward, day and night, on the road in front of the house; however much I tried, there was no chance I could find anything creative to occupy my time. Orange tried the same trick on me by demanding a huge amount of money for a new line. Free could only intervene after Orange – that is France Telecom, who have the monopoly on the national telephone system - had created a new line as there had not been one before, at least not in the last ten years. Living in isolation without internet and a mobile that worked spasmodically, was another reason spirits were not high. So I got a wi-fi router and it seemed to work albeit at a very slow pace. In Languedoc they were beginning to supply optical fibre when I lived here but in Brittany even basic internet was inadequate. I remembered I was given the mobile number of a man who worked for Orange in Vannes by someone who worked in the previous house and so I called him to find out what he could suggest. He was obviously not going to do anything free of charge and it would have to be paid in cash but the practice was not new to me. He told me he would take care of it and I asked for an elucidation. 'Do you mean you will talk to Orange or actually install me a line?'

'I will do what is necessary to give you a line,' he replied.

'And what will the cost be?' I was not in the mood for more bad surprises.

'Nothing. Orange will pay for the work, it is our duty. You will just pay 50 euros for the new line, as normal.'

I could not believe it. Even if I gave him 100 euros in cash, it was still cheaper than the 850 euros Orange demanded. A week later there were men working on the road and fixing the telephone box to the pole; two days later I had telephone and internet. I was so grateful I also bought him a bottle of good Champagne and even though when I handed it to him together with the cash I had the impression he was more into cash than champagne, he seemed to appreciate the gesture. The whole incident confirmed the fact that in Brittany there is a parallel Orange to the official one; a network of swindlers who target foreign clients and blackmail them. I had been with Orange for nearly twelve years and never had a similar experience before notwithstanding the fact that virtually all the houses I moved in required new lines. The Orange man in Vannes was not the talkative type but got things done and how he managed that is a mystery to me. The words 'client' or 'client service' have not always the same significance in France than in other countries. Mainly companies who are principally international have an appreciation of people who regularly contribute to filling their purses, the rest not only do not appreciate but openly disdain the display of affluence, even if it is expended for their benefit. I had met two rich Americans in Tuscany who told me that they went once a year to France and they always stayed in Relais et Châteaux Hotels which are notoriously expensive. At the time the going rate for a suite was 1.500 euros per night; the more they paid, the more they were treated like dirt, they said, so they deleted France from their travelling schedule. But perhaps they expected too much.

Happiness, like its antonym, is a contagious state of being. It is logical that if a region is inhabited by cheerful people, so will be the expatriates living there. All the English people I met in Brittany had the same long faces, woeful eyes and sombre clothing as the Bretons; except Dave and, of course, Yvonne and Kevin. You will think it an exaggeration and you are right, I have been in Brittany a short while and have met very few people. Whilst not ruling out it may have been a coincidence the few I met were a bit morose and perhaps it was that particular area or time of year, it was nevertheless my observation. Having said that, I did meet one or two Bretons who astonished me with their sense of humour - *humor* in French, and it is one of the most difficult words for me to pronounce correctly. One of those was the owner of a DIY store who caters mainly for professional builders and therefore sells large quantities and large containers. I wanted the quality and not the quantity as my requirement was minimal and when he refused to sell me half a sack of fast-acting cement, I exclaimed: 'everything is hard and big here, it really is too much!' And that got him started. Only as I was leaving did I realise what was going through his mind but he did have fun and he made me giggle.

I visited a couple of *vide-greniers* that were held indoors in the summer in contrast with the South where they are outdoor in winter. This kind of event invariably reveals a certain amount of information about the place and the people. You can believe me when I say that I have seen a large number of them all over France and, apart from the fact that the majority sell trash, the trash changes significantly from one department to another. The whole idea behind a *vide-grenier* is exactly that; to dispose of your trash and perhaps buy some other trash that belongs to someone else and then resell it again as trash at another *vide-grenier*. In Brittany they mostly sold old farm tools, dark pieces of furniture and kitchen chattels. Like every place that borders the ocean, its people and places change according to whether they are on the water or inland. The same is for Brittany. Along the coast houses are brighter and people are sunnier. What a difference to be in Quiberon, Locmariaquer or Cancale; the hues are perfect for watercolours and the skies for coloured kites. I went down to Vannes several times and it reminded me of the provençal coast; elegant shops, smartly dressed people and chic restaurants. I went to a dentist in Vannes who was able to turn a tedious visit into a pleasant and jovial encounter and that is not something one finds every day.

France had been united as a country by treaties and invasions and two-thirds of the land has been French for just three hundred and fifty years so an innate sense of national identity had been lacking and it took longer for the Bretons (as well as the Catalans, Flemish and Provençal) to integrate themselves and assume a political identity. Even today the rest of France regards Brittany as a region apart; a place you approach with caution and do not interfere with. We all know about the farmers blocking roads and bringing traffic to a standstill whenever they feel they are unfairly treated by the government. They almost always get what they want; the government knows you do not mess around with a region that supplies your bacon and your potatoes. In fact it provides most of the vegetables to France and its farming, dairy and fish industries are massive; they account for at least 10% of France's national production. Brittany may have experienced poverty in the past but today it is a thriving region. As well as being agriculturally important, Brittany's ports and ship-building industries are equally significant; Brest is the second military port after Toulon and claims to be the largest European centre for maritime science and technology. Unlike the southerners who are known to have a penchant for siestas, Bretons are hard-working and dedicated people.

The leaves were beginning to fall, the walnut tree was dropping walnuts everywhere and the tractors were starting to roll again after a brief summer respite. It was definitely time to go. I was convinced that if I could recuperate the money I put in that house, it would be a miracle. I called the agent who sold it to me and she was full of praises but confirmed the price would barely cover my costs. I could ask a higher price, she said, but it will take longer to sell. I agreed and so as well as giving it to her, I also put an advertisement in leboncoin. For a month and a half only one person called and came to view the house. He was a young chap looking for a large hangar in which to make a workshop but he said there were many more he had to visit and would get in touch later but I knew he would not. Then an email arrived from someone in Biarritz and he made an appointment to come and visit. He said he and his wife loved the photos of the house and it was what they were looking for.

Before they came up to Brittany, they sent his mother to have a shufti and confirm it was what they wanted. The charming woman came from Vannes and repeatedly confirmed it was what her son desired; after she left I knew that was going to be a success. When the couple came to view they were accompanied by her parents who also repeated the property was just perfect for them. And so it went. They had been living in Biarritz for work reasons but wished to return to Brittany, where they actually came from. They, Elise and Michael, were simply wonderful and the kindest people one could ever meet. An added bonus was the fact that we communicated almost exclusively in English as they speak it perfectly. They could not have closed my chapter in Brittany with a more positive and uplifting note. I always meant to light a candle in thanks for this little miracle, a symbol of my gratitude for not despairing and believing that there is always a light in dark places.

I knew exactly where I wanted to move to next; Languedoc. Am I a glutton for punishment? Perhaps. The reason for this decision was that after the farming and the breeding what I needed was hills, olive groves and vineyards and in the absence of Tuscany, Languedoc was the next best thing. At the beginning I looked at Midi-Pyrénées and specifically the Aveyron but it is known to be damp and that is one of the things I was escaping from. In Languedoc I have friends and as the saying 'third time lucky' came to my mind, I was sure it could not be another disaster. Mike, a friend I had met in Languedoc some years back and has since also moved to Brittany, had introduced me to Linda and John who live near Narbonne and they have become two additional friends I now have in Languedoc. One of the projects that were pencilled in my mind was to go and look at Spain since I know nothing of that country, except what I have read. But life seems to present me with an endless sequence of engagements and tasks; or perhaps it is me who crafts them. It is still on the agenda and now that I live fairly close to Spain, I should take the time to go and see also that amazing nation. It is curious how certain countries attract us and others not at all; what is it that makes a Parisian want to live in Florence, a Japanese settle down in Manchester or an Australian buy a house in a French forgotten village? Perhaps not everything can be explained away scientifically as it is being done at the moment by technical experts; perhaps there are elements in all of us that elude scientific laws and patterns. Something that is not measurable or quantifiable.

THINGS CHANGE TO STAY THE SAME

The Return of The Jedi

I have a friend who is a Buddhist Monk and he is also a Kendo Master. I would have liked to learn the Art though I have never asked him to teach me and do not know if he would have acquiesced. When we have a conversation, it is almost always on the subject of liberating oneself and finding inner peace, being the only place it can be found. For someone like me who has been and is extremely itinerant, meditation has been essential in keeping myself in line with myself and focus on what is important in each single moment. When will you find peace, someone asked. Had I been more present I would have answered that you cannot find something that you already have; it is a question of connecting to it rather than seeking it. Everything is already and always there, it is only a matter of connection. Each of us can have an understanding of something proportionally dependent on our acumen and self-knowledge. It is like having glasses through which one can see two, three or seven-dimensionally; the views will be significantly different and yet each person looking through the glasses is convinced of looking at reality. In my student days in London I was a member of an esoteric society in which all sorts of subjects were researched and studied. After seven years, I thought I knew everything that is important. I left to travel the world and put my learning to the test; today I often ask myself the question: do I really learn, and what do I learn?

As I was making my way down to the South from Brittany, it was that question I was asking myself in the car along the way; what did I learn from my previous experiences in Languedoc? One has to be fairly robust to deal with the fiery and strident character of the locals and one never knows what goes on behind closed doors, whether they are physical doors or in one's mind. What I have noted is that in the South one makes instant friends – at least superficially – but then suddenly finds they have gone with the wind. It is like someone who lets you into their house, not the whole house but just the entrance, to have a close look at you and judge whether you are allowed to move into the next room. So better not get excited about their initial burst of hospitality as it may be their last. How they manage to judge and decide is an enigma. It is not a very good paradigm but hopefully it conveys the idea. On the other hand in the North – Brittany for example – people do not let you into the entrance at all, they have to feel you and study you first but once they have decided to let you in, it is unlikely they will change their minds and let you out.

Where I live now is between Limoux and Carcassonne. It is a small village with enough British residents to make it interesting and enjoyable. It was shown to me on a windy day by an agent who did not believe she would make a sale that day. I knew it from her eyes. But I surprised her. Before finding the village I asked a woman in Saint-Hilaire if she could point me in the right direction and she did; she also added 'I hope you will come to live here, my name is Suzanne.' I have since had the pleasure of becoming more acquainted with this lovely woman and hope we will become friends. In a way I was so relieved to have returned to the South that my expectations and priorities had moved in the background. I wanted the hills, the olives and the vineyards and here they are. I did not expect to find a welcome but I got it and that made quite a difference. The house was inexpensive, the works required were minimal (except the façade) and I have a nice view from my terrace; what more can one want?

The *petite maison* had been renovated by an Englishman who did a lot of work himself, if not all in fact. There were still things to be done but plumbing and electricity were new. I have never met him as the contract was signed with power of attorney but everyone tells me he is a delightful person and I am sure he is. As I was repainting the front door and generally improving the house, people would come and introduce themselves which was a normal thing enough but had never happened to me before. That made me feel accepted - though I knew full well one should be cautious about having such premature feelings – and thought that perhaps I had finally earned the right to be treated like a human being. Some of them proceeded to tell me about others in the village whom I knew nothing about; they told me what their qualities and faults were (according to their personal opinions) and generally gossip about others. It is impossible to find a village where people never gossip, being the oldest and most widely practised tradition in the world, (apart from prostitution) but it is not one I care for. One of these persons was a woman who told me she was into the business of teaching people how to run their lives and generally healing them but she also showed signs of being a tattler and a narcissist, seeing that her monologue about herself took up all the space. I wanted to tell her that if you claim to be an authority on how people should live their lives, you have to live yours in line with impeccable ethics and be a living model of your teaching – but I did not.

By this time people have already formed in their minds a vague portrait of who I am, or rather how they see me. It is indispensable for them to put people into a frame, even if it is just to show that they do not fit into the frame. They have no idea who I am, where I come from or what I have done but that will not stop them putting me into a neat little configuration that makes them feel secure. Then they discover little bits about a person, fragments of a composition that they cannot place together. It is beyond their understanding and so they are unable to form a concrete assessment; they are then forced to accept that person because being unable to label them, they cannot like or dislike them. And that is the advantage in being unpredictable. Once upon a time I learned to play the piano (badly) and when I found out there is someone in the village who has two, I thought, what can I do to get in that woman's good graces? Then it transpired I had some things she wanted and instead of receiving money I could have proposed to play the piano once in a while; say once a month. But no, she did not want the fabric and alas she never invited me to play the piano. But then, everyone is free to do what they want with their piano or their forte.

The house is now completely done, including the façade. I have used the local artisans who have been exceptional. I try to make myself useful, I give things I have when I see people need them, I do the shopping for a couple of aged people who cannot drive and I have been inspired to paint and write. The locals are incredibly friendly and respectful which is most auspicious. In particular I have met some lovely people who have befriended me; Mary and David, Natalie, Kim and Nigel; they are all marvellous and hope our friendships will survive along our journeys. Mel is finally able to display his sociability as there are plenty of friendly dogs in the village – Jack, the Basset Hound, is his favourite pal – and there are also plenty of cats but Mel has developed a certain tolerance; perhaps he finally understands it is a losing battle with them. The amazing thing is that people ask me if he is a puppy or a very young dog when in fact he is nearly ten years old. He seems to never age (to my regret!) as on the contrary I do. He must be a canine Peter Pan, I tell myself. My social life, like that of my dog, has also livened up a little but I still find enough time to be with myself, which is vitally important.

This is probably not the last place I will have moved to but I would like to think the wind is at my back sufficiently for me to finish my next book on Tuscany and, who knows, finally print the final chapters on my long-awaited novel. In my calculations I have, up to now, paid over 65.000 euros to the French State in taxes due to all the houses I bought and sold. I have renovated some dilapidated places along the way, paid agents, artisans, removers, notaries, DIY stores and donated other unquantifiable things. I pay my private medical insurance and have enriched vets all over the country. At this point, after 12 years of moving, despite all the money I have willingly bestowed, I am left with a little bit more than what I had when I gave up my work and came to France. That was my aim at the beginning and that is what I have done. I do not ask for any gratitude, award or compensation but I do wish that people come to their senses and stop judging me unstable and restless simply because they lack discernment. We ought to get to know others before pronouncing judgments and avoid passing them on to more people who only contribute to aggravate them until they become time bombs.

It has been an enjoyable journey despite all the problems and stressful situations; the physical, mental and emotional fatigue. Everyone I have interrelated with has taught me something; the experience has certainly been an initiation. I have met new friends along the way; Sheena from Ireland, Philip from Italy, Roberta and Daniele Rampini from Italy, Olga, Gaston, Anne, Beatrice from Vaucluse; Nadia and Bertrand from Provence, Bernard from La Rochelle. And of course Laura with her little Archie who loved Mel like a brother and vice versa. Some I may only have met once but there is an invisible empathic thread that keeps us connected and I am grateful for their friendship. Surviving the voyage and coming out of it un-damaged, has given me added confidence and liberty. This has been my way of doing it for a time and may not be everyone's but whatever one choses to do, it is important to remember that obstacles are often self-created and finding solutions to problems is more effective and rewarding than being conditioned by the problems. I think loving what we do is the most important thing and the key to being successful in what we do.

ACKNOWLEDGEMENTS

I would like to thank Suzanne Fox, Mary, David, Kim and Nigel Sibley and Mike for reading my draft and being so encouraging and positive.

I have told the truth – as I know it – and if in the process I have offended anyone, it has not been my intention and you have my apologies.

Everything in this book has been designed by me and belongs to me, including all the photos.

Printed in Great Britain
by Amazon